Croatia

**Travels in
Undiscovered
Country**

Croatia

Travels in
Undiscovered
Country

Tony Fabijančić

THE UNIVERSITY OF ALBERTA PRESS

Published by

The University of Alberta Press
Ring House 2
Edmonton, Alberta T6G 2E1

NATIONAL LIBRARY OF CANADA CATALOGUING IN PUBLICATION DATA

Fabijancic, Tony, 1966–
    Croatia : travels in undiscovered country / Tony Fabijancic.

    Includes bibliographical references and index.
    ISBN 0–88864–397–7

    1. Fabijancic, Tony, 1966– —Journeys—Croatia. 2. Croatia—Description and travel.
I. Title.
DR1517.F32 2003   914.97204'3   C2002–911032–7

Printed and bound in Canada by Kromar Printing Ltd., Winnipeg.

Printed on acid-free paper.

Copyediting by Christine Savage.

Publication assistance by Tara Taylor.

Book design by Carol Dragich.

The University of Alberta Press acknowledges the financial support of the Government
of Canada through the Book Publishing Industry Development Program for its
publishing activities. The Press also gratefully acknowledges the support received for its
program from the Canada Council for the Arts.

THE CANADA COUNCIL | LE CONSEIL DES ARTS
FOR THE ARTS | DU CANADA
SINCE 1957 | DEPUIS 1957

This book is for my family—
past, present, and yet to come.

■ CONTENTS

Who would fardels bear,
To grunt and sweat under a weary life,
But that the dread of something after death,
The undiscovered country, from whose bourn
No traveller returns, puzzles the will
And makes us rather bear those ills we have,
Than fly to others that we know not of?
Thus conscience does make cowards of us all,
And thus the native hue of resolution
Is sicklied o'er with the pale cast of thought,
And enterprises of great pith and moment,
With this regard, their currents turn awry,
And lose the name of action.

—William Shakespeare, *Hamlet*

I remember my youth and the feeling that will never
come back anymore—the feeling that I could last
forever, outlast the sea, the earth, and all men; the
deceitful feeling that lures us on to joys, to perils, to
love, to vain effort—to death; the triumphant
conviction of strength, the heat of life in the handful of
dust, the glow in the heart that with every year grows
dim, grows cold, grows small, and expires—and
expires too soon, too soon—before life itself.

—Joseph Conrad, "Youth"

■ PREFACE

I WANTED TO WRITE A TRAVEL BOOK AFTER READING Patrick Leigh Fermor's record of his journey on foot from Holland to Hungary in the 1930s, *A Time of Gifts*. So, in 1996, I headed off on my own arduous walk, through the coastal regions of my father's homeland, Croatia.

I almost didn't go. Jobless, convinced I should act responsibly and find work in Vancouver where my father lived, I was set to make another epic journey across Canada by car. It would be my fifth such journey—the first with my family when we emigrated from Alberta to the Maritimes, then four others in my eleven-year chase of three degrees. The night before leaving my mother's house in Nova Scotia, I turned sleeplessly like one of those roasting chickens in a grocery store. Thousands of kilometres and months of responsibility stretched ahead. True, I'd been inured to responsibility and discipline as long as I could remember, but now the qualities that partly made me who I was seemed antagonistic. Besides, I hadn't taken an extended holiday for years; right after finishing my PhD, when I should have sunk into a period of hedonism, I got my first teaching contract in western

Newfoundland. The following spring, I wanted to relax, feel the sun on my face. and enjoy some of the little money I'd eked out. I wanted to explore my own roots after feeling displaced for so long. A week after that sleepless night, I was tramping down the Adriatic.

Looking back, I suppose the sun and sea drew me to the coast as much as any legitimate claim about my roots there. After all, my father was born in the northern region of Prigorje, and although my family and I took holidays in various resorts over the years, we never stayed longer than a week at a time. But in my mind, Croatia's Adriatic was also part of me—and seemed a richer subject for travel writing than the rest of the country. How wrong I turned out to be.

Driven to return home like a horse to its stable (as my mother put it), my father kept my links to Croatia alive. Growing up in Edmonton, I remember him dragging us to Croatian picnics, playing soccer with the senior teams he coached, and roasting pigs in our suburban backyard. Still, I didn't think of myself as a Croat; Yugoslavia was the "old country" for me, if not for my father. I had no real understanding of the country's history, nor feelings of nationalism. All that changed with the demise of Yugoslavia in the early 1990s, when Croatia as an entity became a reality for me. I learned more, watched a dozen news broadcasts a day at the height of the war, and wrote articles defending Croatia's position. I became a Croatian Canadian.

So while my book began as a writing holiday, it also began with cultural undertones. Then during a momentous trip down the Adriatic highway and to the island of Pag, everything began to change. Not only did I confront the material reality of distances and Croatia's summer sun (it was hot! and I knew it would beat me), but when I got to the town of Pag itself and saw what there was to see, I had my first and only epiphany of its kind, intensified by the ancient world around me: the pressing reality about this "bower of bone" that Jesuit poet Gerard Manley Hopkins called the body. In the very moment when I basked in my freedom, strength and youth, I understood intimately, viscerally, that it would all be taken away.

Instead of being defeated, I found more energy. I wanted to see and do more—to act, not contemplate. A book about the Adriatic coast alone would be incomplete, I realized, because it wouldn't represent Croatia's extraordinary regionality. What's more, I didn't know much about Prigorje itself, not even about the valley next to the one where my father was born. I wanted to find out more. Thus, I obviated my frailty on the road by aspiring to the whole country's truth, which meant travelling further faster (than my legs would allow).

And so the book grew. My journey eventually took me (by foot, bicycle, tram, bus, car, ferry, and plane) from the nine-hundred-year-old capital, Zagreb, through the peasant regions of Prigorje, Zagorje, and Slavonia, to the Adriatic coast, the frontier territories of Krajina and Herzegovina, and the Istrian peninsula. Although these journeys took place from 1996 to 1999, I've gone further back into Croatia's past, and into my own. I've spent years all told in some parts of the country and only hours (or less) in others. The essays in this book reflect those experiences: on the one hand, unhurried travel ruminations in which I talk about a way of life I know well and from the inside, and on the other, sketches more aptly reflecting a foreigner's perspective. Indeed, I see myself as part native and part outsider simultaneously, which allows me a particular perspective on the country.

Generally, the chapters parallel my travels from north to south, but occasionally I've veered from this format for thematic reasons. For instance, I begin with Pag in order to emphasize its symbolic weight in my imagination and to index Croatia's identity as my own "undiscovered country," from which I returned changed forever. Hamlet's contemplation of death as a domain from "whose bourn no traveller returns" is also applicable to Croatia—literally—since over the centuries it was often a site of war and death, a place from where many people, including travellers, never returned. Croatia is also an undiscovered country in a different sense. It's at a propitious moment when the world of peasants, shepherds, and fishermen is dying, irrevocably giving way to the new reality of a modern European state—when its former fabric is unravelling forever. Croatia is more and more undiscovered, in this sense, since its old ways are increasingly disappearing within the rising tableau of the new. It was my purpose, therefore, to document this change by discovering hidden corners of the country about which even Croats seemed uninterested.

I haven't written a nostalgic ethnography, a history book, or a journalistic travel book in which the landscape becomes the occasion for a mainly political and historical documentation, although there is some of that here. I haven't written about modern Croatia, or about every single region, cultural monument, historical personality, or issue deemed important by the experts. I've emphasized facts of a different order: the evanescent moment on the road that captured, nevertheless, the spirit of the old world still in evidence; the hidden or forgotten "crevices"; the personal instead of the public; and the present still permeated by a vital past.

■ ACKNOWLEDGEMENTS

I AM GRATEFUL TO ALL THE PEOPLE ASSOCIATED with the University of Alberta Press for understanding the spirit of the book I wrote and guiding it expertly to its final form.

Earlier versions of some sections appeared in *The Antigonish Review* and the *Globe and Mail*. Thank you to George Sanderson and Trevor Cole for their interest and support.

I received funds from Sir Wilfred Grenfell College, Memorial University of Newfoundland, covering travel and photographic costs. Librarians and staff also provided help in gathering research and physically assembling the manuscript. Thank you also to Kim MacDonald and Joanne Bouchard at St. Francis Xavier University for computer assistance and for scanning the photographs.

My thanks are also due to Vlado Juranko and Bryan Hall for their insights about political figures and events, and to Mike Nolan for his jaunts to the QE II Library in St. John's.

I must take responsibility for any outstanding mistakes in the book, but many were detected by Ursula Panzer, Teodora Hictaler, and Natasha Fabijančić. Thank you Uschi for long hours of editing, and Tea for rigorous collation and translation.

Finally I am indebted to the people of Croatia and Herzegovina who allowed me into their homes, gave me food and drink, and told me about their lives. Without their hospitality and trust I could never have written this book.

■ A NOTE ON THE TEXT

I HAVE ANGLICISED SOME SPELLINGS BECAUSE THEY are familiar to English speakers (Slavonia, not *Slavonija*; Yugoslavia, not *Jugoslavija*). Some words are familiar in their original so I have kept their spellings (Krajina). But I have preferred to let others, which are often Anglicised (Chetnik, Ustasha), stand in their original form (Četnik, Ustaša). Except for proper nouns, words in languages other than English are italicised. English rules regarding capitalization are followed throughout (Krvavi Most, not *Krvavi most*). As for the difference between "Croat" and "Croatian," I have chosen the former to denote individuals and ethnicity, and the latter mainly to denote the language, linguistic issues, or matters of state. At times, I have abandoned this pattern if it struck me as awkward in a particular context.

The Croatian language includes a number of unfamiliar letters in English. Ones used in this book are listed below.

c – *ts*, as in ca*ts*
č – *ch*, as in *ch*ur*ch*
ć – like *ch*, but softer, as in fu*t*ure
j – *y*, as in *y*esterday
š – *sh*, as in *sh*ip
ž – *zh*, as in trea*s*ure

◪ INTRODUCTION

CROATIA (HRVATSKA) IS AN ANCIENT NATION, YET a very young nation state. Once a formidable kingdom under Tomislav in the tenth century, a naval power in the sixteenth and seventeenth, and an awakening national entity in the nineteenth, it had to endure a thousand years of foreign meddling, subjugation, incursions, and outright wars before being recognized in 1992 as a distinct entity.

Small but complex, roughly 56,000 kilometres square with a population of 4.8 million, Croatia is located south of Austria and Hungary, between Slovenia and Bosnia-Herzegovina, and along the Adriatic Sea, which it shares with Italy. Croatia's northern plains and hills, its isolated Dinaric interior, and its coast, consisting of more than a thousand islands, sixty-six said to be inhabited, make up its three geographical regions, which have thwarted unity, impeded and facilitated invasions, and resulted in ties with central Europe, southern Europe, and the east. Croatia is a culturally rich country of architectural wonders and natural beauty, venerable traditions, and a long, deep past. Its history is violent and labyrinthine, and its regions are so varied that attitudes and dialects change, and women tie their kerchiefs differently from one valley to another.

Map of Croatia.

Croatia is usually included within the geographical parameters of the Balkan peninsula, but most Croats don't consider Croatia a Balkan nation at all, pointing out its long history within the orbit of western influence—eight hundred years for its northern regions within the Hungarian, Austrian and Austro-Hungarian Empires, for example. Yet those who make this argument also say that Croatia always strained under the yoke of "imperialist" western power—that it never belonged spiritually, ideologically, or linguistically, that it was different. This contradiction lies at the heart of the problematic identity of the new Croatia, which emerged in 1991. Some Croats claim that the country is western (and therefore not Balkan) and yet distinct, thereby perilously approaching the "Other" of Balkan Slavic identity. But the Croat peasant has more in common with his Serb counterpart, who essentially speaks the same language and shares some of the same attitudes, than with the Croat intellectual who dispels such similarities.

But what is Balkan? Discussion of this term, of course, can be neither conclusive nor satisfactory. A Croat friend of mine once joked that it's something "really really bad." True, it has usually been used pejoratively to describe a primitive, violent tribal *gestalt* applicable to all ethnic groups of the region, the residual economic backwardness left by the Ottoman Empire, and a rock-hard resistance to modern democratic political processes, all of which grow more noticeable the further east one travels. Any superficial glance at the country in its first ten years suggests that Croatia wasn't entirely western, at least not in typically accepted political or economic terms, given its corrupt and troubled transition to capitalism and democracy. More stores, fancy cars, and big money are other cosmetic changes that don't automatically make a country civilized, modern, and "not Balkan." But corruption in politics and the switch from socialism to capitalism aren't restricted only to the former Yugoslavia.

What about the people? My trips in rural Croatia, even through its major cities, showed me that it occupies zone territory between so-called western and Balkan influences. For me, this doesn't only mean that Croats exhibit traces of the west and east in their lives, that they drink both cappuccino and Turkish coffee, but that their particular *gestalt* precludes clear categorization within these polarities. Farming villages inevitably contrast successful operations run by upstanding, "gentlemen" farmers on the one hand, and careless, more primitive, even slovenly, destitution headed by patriarchs who, if described accurately, make the outsider seem a condescending, anti-Balkan bigot, but who are real nonetheless.

The answers to Croat identity lie somewhere between those contraries. If Balkan can't be defined, then Croat seems more determinable, especially if pursued in material detail.

PAG
Bower of Bone

CROATIA'S HIGHWAY FROM ISTRIA TO DUBROVNIK is a heat-cracked grey line unspooling along the blue waves of the Velebit Mountains. At ten in the morning, the sun is burning me as I zigzag along the road in search of shade from olive trees and stone walls, while every so often a car rips past into the heat lines. In the summer of 1996, the coast is deserted because tourists are still afraid to die in a war zone.

I'm on the way to the ferry bound for the island of Pag—only an hour's walk south from the terminal for Rab, I was told. But with Prizna nowhere in sight and the feverish sun filling my head, I realize I've overstretched myself. As fast as cars come, they're gone, and I'm alone again. The only sounds are my steps on the hot concrete and the soft mewing of seagulls on my left. They slide on air currents in slow revolutions, an elegant, floating dance. To my right and far below are the pearly Kvarner Islands in the cuttingly bright blue sea. It's beautiful here, desolate and still.

Although this casual jaunt down the coast is unnerving, I can still joke to myself about the soldiers' memorial stones that are cemented into walls along the road. Not my time yet, I figure. When the Prizna sign looks like it will never appear and no car will ever drive by again and the heat is too much to bear, a rusted white Rabbit grinds up the hill toward me. Not believing my good luck, I see it stop a few metres ahead and I get in.

The guy staring me down is a hulking, black-haired army corporal with dense eyebrows and a hooked nose, which give him a predatory look. His sallow cheeks are covered by tufts of hair and his right thumb looks like it was melted off and stuck back on. Although he's on his way to the mainland port city of Zadar, about fifty kilometres south of Pag, he offers to detour with me across the island and even covers the cost of the ferry. He doesn't mind delaying the return to his wife and kids, even though he hasn't seen them in three months. It makes me wonder what reasons he really has for driving me down some forsaken stretch of road.

We take off and, ten minutes later, rattle down the steep turnoff to the ferry stop and onto a rusted carcass of a boat. We leave the car and climb aboard the platform that rings the ferry. Across the Velebitski Kanal, Pag's ominously barren white tail is submerged in the sea. The island looks desolate on the mainland side: no trees, no shelter, no life.

"See this," the corporal growls, pointing to a scar on the back of his left arm. "Serb sniper almost got me. Lucky I moved at the last second." He glances at the water, then back at me. "I was carrying a howitzer so I pointed it at the fucker and killed him." His face freezes into a smile and goosebumps spring up on his arms. "Boom," he adds.

Christ! The world around us disappears, and I feel jailed in his moment, in his presence—dark eyes, dark smile. Then he's on to something else and just as quickly he seems OK. I once knew another Croat like this, but he never made it to the war. He died accidentally from a gunshot to the chest, fired by a drunken friend. Ivek Jacopač was nicknamed The Moth for fluttering around bars late at night—a Casanova type with slickly combed brown hair and brown eyes that always met another's without flinching. He used to drive his dad's twenty-five-year-old John Deere in his dress pants and patent leather shoes, searching from village to village for some cheap fix. One day he stacked wood for my friend's parents in exchange for some dinars and a meal. He had a loud voice and seemed to know a thing or two. He ate quickly, ripping chunks of bread from the loaf to dunk in his soup and goulash, then eased back in his chair and finished off the decanter of wine. He was never openly contemptuous of me but I know he was. "Forget university," he told me that day. "The only real education is the education of life." Ivek Jacopač—educated at thirty-five.

The ferry trip lasts twenty minutes and soon Pag rises up in front of us, a bone-coloured moonscape cut above the ferry terminal by a forty-five-degree road winding tiredly up through the rock. Sun and wind seem to have cracked the white hills with hammer blows. There's no vegetation here, but soon we enter a more hospitable region where the land slopes down to the emerald sea and hip-high evergreen maquis is sprinkled between the island's white shards of rock. Fig and olive trees scattered here and there are bent away from the white coast like stooped old men. Stone walls, some piled centuries ago, rope down the island like security for cargo when the Bura blows in the winter. Off the coast and rising mysteriously from the haze of heat are the little islands of Škrda and Maun, far away yet seemingly close enough to touch—a paradox that always belongs to the sea's illusion of immeasurable distance and space.

And then there is the wind: warm blasts of it through our open windows, blowing swallows across the sky and the aroma of curry from some herb. What beautiful desolation! I try to absorb every detail, as if each were precious and must be sealed by memory. Quiet for a bit, as if he's sensitive to my impressions, the corporal smiles at me. I catch him glancing now and again at the sights. The motor is humming smoothly and the road stretches in front of us, rising eventually to a summit from which the village of Povljana is just visible, a distant scattering of orange and white.

Finally we cut through an opening at the top of the island and descend sharply toward Pag, which lies between mountain ridges at the southeast end of a long bay. At two in the afternoon, the place is simmering in the heat. I say goodbye to my driver, thanking him for his generosity and ashamed of my suspicions. Sorry to see him go in the end, I head to a nearby café that overlooks Pag's heat-bright rooftops.

I dump my pack and have a beer as I gaze across town at the white hills down which we just drove, at villas dotting the coast and greenery fingering halfway to the top. Somehow the combination of stone emptiness and pockets of green life along a pristine blue sea distinguishes the place and makes it more beautiful. The spareness has seduced me—this sparse, elemental world without vegetative finery or excess, the bare bones of the planet's life.

A short walk to the market and down a cobblestone street lined every ten yards by brown and green wooden doors eventually takes me to Pag's spacious main square. Laid out in 1443 by permission of Venetian Doge Francesco Foscari, according to plans initially drawn by Juraj Dalmatinac (familiar in Italy as Giovanni da Trau, whose Šibenik cathedral is among his many masterworks), Pag was built in grid formation with two main streets meeting at right angles, dividing the town in four. A nearly empty café waits for the summer crowd, and from the shady streets women trudge slowly into the heat on various errands. So far, there's not a man to be seen.

After stopping at a deli for a smoked sausage and *paški sir* (ewe's cheese), I leave the square and soon find myself at the stone dock, where a tall ship under repair is moored. Three or four cafés bordered by squat palm trees are host to half the male population of the town—men finished work for the afternoon, drinking and smoking. Some look grizzled enough to be actual fishermen; others are middle-aged shop owners who've closed their doors for the afternoon, and the rest are young locals starting to party early this Friday.

Looking down the line of cafés, Pag bay lies to the left, and the sand-and-pebble beach arcs elegantly into the distance. Another short walk takes me away from the dock and back into the narrow streets where locals are starting to gather on their small steps. Little pizzerias, ice cream and jewellery shops, shining with polished granite and brass and oak, are secreted among the old buildings like oases of enterprise.

In the evening, old men tidily dressed in blue or white pressed shirts and grey or brown slacks chat on wooden benches at the dock,

A street in Pag, 1996.

and the cafés hum with loud, throb-bassed Europop. Girls are flitting around in brightly coloured flocks, and boys on mountain bikes circle the town in quick, aggressive swoops.

I can't distinguish the lot of them from young people anywhere in Europe, although there seems to be a uniqueness to their dark, sullen beauty—something in their eyes, in the shrill or growling command in their voices. Even at a young age, the boys have already acquired the gestural and vocal mastery that characterizes many Croat men, and the girls, as a form of response, have evolved something of the same, with which they compete.

Some things will never change, only die. In the streets just after dark, under light bulbs stuck out of walls, old women dressed all in black, comically rotund but somehow frightening and even demonic, gather in coteries of two to disclose secretly the day's news or remember some collective history lived long ago and now forgotten by everyone but them. These black pairs roost on the back streets away from the square and dock where Pag's life centres—that energy youthful by contrast, two contraries like magnetic poles repelling each other.

■

Cottony clouds blown by gentle winds are rolling shadows across the distant hills, but the bay is a motionless turquoise mirror. It's very hot, so the sea is tremendously cooling. Except for some high-school students escaping for the day, I'm by myself on the beach. June is a magical time when the Adriatic coast still projects a mysterious charge and a sharp sense of the past. But already there are signs of the coming tourist onslaught as well as the new times—big shots from Zagreb, their eyes lidded by black sunglasses, idling along the docks in their Mercedes. A German motorboat is carving up the bay. Old and new are becoming inextricably entwined in the tapestry of independent Croatia.

For now, the past is all around and still living. Every afternoon, the same old women who hang around after dark sit on chairs in the streets and sew intricate pieces of *čipka* (lace), their finished work displayed like big snowflakes in the windows of their houses. These women, with their white and grey hair done up in buns and their black skirts draped almost to the ground and their feet in slippers, are alike enough to look like variants of a single model built by some puppet-maker long ago. The old women seem surprised when they see me, as if they consider travellers some alien phenomenon. For a few seconds I feel I'm offering them a unique glimpse into a foreign world.

But I'm wrong, of course. These women are not quite so naïve, nor are they such romantic figures. While they belong to Pag's past and their art is very old, they've also been selling it for years, long before the new spirit of enterprise. Chances are they think the season's too young for tourists, so I'm an anomaly, a curiosity. And not a very rich one at that.

Some people here aren't interested in making money. Ive Meštrović is a retired fisherman I meet as he's trying his luck off the dock beside

Wooden boat on Pag beach, 1996.

the tall ship. In a clean white shirt rolled up at the sleeves, grey slacks, and suspenders, he walks the length of the promenade all the way to the moored skiffs and back, leading a line coiled around a wooden stick. The little flat *stočarski* he catches, which rise glittering and quivering to the surface from the bottom of the evening-dark green harbour, are all too small, so he tosses them back. He looks at me only once and quickly through his thick lenses, his brown eyes sad and watery. From then on he focusses on his work.

"Those hills there," he begins, not answering a question but responding intuitively to some interest I must have been showing by watching him, "used to be all vineyards. Around 1965. Now there's mostly hotels or villas, old people dead and young ones too lazy to work, selling out." Another fish leaps out of the water on the shining line. He peers at it a second, then unhooks it and lets it go. The bells from Pag's parish church are chiming eight o'clock and the sun is setting over the mountainsides of the bay. The light is beautiful, coppery, and the wind is whispering around us. "I come here now," he says with an almost embarrassed shrug, "to spend a little time."

He becomes quiet as he works on his line and doesn't seem to notice me anymore, so I leave him with his thoughts and his fish.

■

This is my last night. On my final walk, I find myself in front of a big church, Uznesenje Marijino (The Assumption, 1443–1448), which stands rather unspectacularly in the main square, hardly distinguishable from the other buildings, with its cream-white façade and block-like structure.

What's most intriguing about this church is its interior. Hexagonal pulpits and Gothic chapels at the end of each aisle bookend the dark inner space of the church. The floors of the chapels are inlaid with the marble sarcophagi of clerics whose names and dates etched in the stone have nearly been rubbed out by the centuries' tread of parishioners, like rough objects smoothened by water. Built into the floors and walls are black and white marble skull and crossbones, polished and cackling menacingly in the half-light. They are ferocious, especially in a church where Christ's gentle image is scattered around. Then there are the gorgeously patterned mauve marble pillars holding the structure up, and on the Baroque ceiling three medallions showing St. George and the Dragon, the Assumption, and the martyrdom of St. Sebastian. Though quiet now in the evening, only echoing a little coldly when I walk, the place seems eerily alive with long-ago sermons and hymns.

Stepping outside into the evening, I feel a difference. The living world suddenly projects a haunting immateriality, bodies blown away into a million scattered dots that once made the picture whole. The wind is singing through the narrow corridors and shadowy figures are breaking up in the town's darkening spaces. Only the first few steps are unreal, and then the flagstones start to press up against my feet and I feel my weight again. As lights come on, I wander around town to take in the meaning of the last few minutes. Such an old place like Pag will enforce its age on the psyche in one way or another, especially forcefully on a Canadian for whom time has never been so apparent in his country's architecture. A strange combination of tangible fear and freedom has coalesced powerfully in these few seconds and will never recur so strongly. My youth is over because I've flashed ahead, felt a hot current surge through me, been electrified to my end. I'm amazed this flash of eternity hasn't scarred me forever with fear. But I don't care. These legs still work and these hands still move.

Here on the edges of Croatia, I make a decision to explore the rest of the country, beginning in the urban centre from which journeys outward are journeys into the past, and where statements about the disappearing world are inflected by greater poignancy. There the peasant is an increasingly marginal figure. There the gap between new and old is sharper, marked by residual traces and a city's nostalgia.

2 ◼ ZAGREB
The Transformed City

SIX MONTHS HAVE PASSED SINCE MY TRIP TO PAG. I've become attuned to time reified in the oldest buildings, though I feel more and more that this sense of permanence is an illusion and evidence of my Canadian origins. Even the oldest buildings and the meanings attributed to them change, as do the people who built them or used them, their ideologies and customs. While I was changed in a way I didn't expect, and while I'm on the lookout for the past inscribed around me, I've also started searching for signs of the opposite—for impermanence beyond my own, for the ebbing of time out of things. This waning, which is the present moment, is everywhere visible to me in a big city like Zagreb.

It's December 1996, five years after Croatia's self-declared independence. Some people are still wearing clothing out of the Yugoslav era: woollen great coats with big 1970s collars, plastic-looking leather jackets, polyester winter coats that look like they were fabricated in a state factory somewhere. Amid this working class are handsome young people who have gone to the other extreme and are dressed very fashionably.

I'm riding tram number 12 from Ljubljanica station to Zagreb's centre at Ban Jelačić Square. The wood panelling inside apparently aspired to sports-car chic but now is cracked and stained. All three cars are jammed with people, and at every stop a few more squeeze in before the doors clap shut.

At first this is the grey city of Croatia's Yugoslav years. The buildings are dark apartment rows with businesses at street level: grocery stores and cafés, tawdry jewellery and clothing shops, drab hair salons named after women like Jasna or Jadranka. Black graffiti deface the walls, including the ubiquitous tag of someone called Emil.

This Zagreb hasn't changed one iota. The more I look around, the more I understand what some writers mean when they say that communism may have preserved a Balkan ambience.[1] Yet this periphery of Zagreb can't be conveniently labelled "Balkan" in order to give it an essence distinguishable from "western" or "European" or "modern." That's because there's nothing essential about it, since it's mostly the product of a specific economic and political system that designed it, built it, and let it grow dingy.

If the epithet "Balkan" can be applied usefully to people, then - people I see don't exemplify the term's uncouth connotations. They look busy: they're walking, carrying, lifting, stacking, unloading, piling, sweeping, bartering, arguing, talking, laughing, gesturing. No peasants are on the streets, no beggars, drunks, addicts, suspicious characters, prophets, pimps, or hookers; indeed, one has to visit a surprisingly long time to catch a sight of this *lumpenproletariat*. I see shoppers in open-air markets and at kiosks, women kissing in greeting and strolling away arm in arm, and men exchanging currency outside banks and selling newspapers between lanes at stoplights. I know that many people here attend mass, choose generous presents for godchildren, honour saints' days, names' days, and hold enormous weddings that last all night. In their many cafés, they drink the same soft drinks found anywhere in the west, European and local beers, but also wine spritzers called *gemišt*, as well as *šljivovica, loza, viljamovka*, and other brandies.

On a visit to Yugoslavia in 1987, I was driven by my cousin through the bleak urban blight of new Zagreb to a concert celebrating 1970s Yugo rock. For a kid who grew up in Canadian suburbia, the scene was unreal. It was a gothic biker-gang Woodstock. There were balding, ponytailed aesthetes dressed in black leather who toked on joints and looked like they lived on a diet of bad air. Disaffected students in black coats assembled in groups, evidence of reports that a nihilistic cult called the Crna Ruža (Black Rose) had been founded, a group of people who read Baudelaire and Nietzsche and held ritual suicides. Greasers in biker jackets and ducktailed haircuts filed into the bunker. Everyone was smoking. Cigarette and marijuana smoke, so thick it was a tangible substance we waded through, nearly drowned the stage and blotted out the lighters hundreds of fans waved during ballads. Some of the music was hard rock so loud and thrashy I enjoyed it. It seemed to suggest a social chaos just under the communist façade.

These social or fashion codes are gone forever. But for me, they belong tangentially to an almost undefinable quality still apparent in Zagreb's urban periphery—beyond fashion, in some people's bodies, something brooding and sallow even in their gazes. Even though fans at the concert affected the gestures of rebellion against this sullen fatalism (as I could begin to define it), they were also inadvertently complicit with it. As is probably the case elsewhere in eastern Europe, this quality could be some trace of communism rather than anything inherently Balkan. Yet I also see a bodily rhetoric that doesn't originate in communism. The mastery I also noticed in Pag is a confident bluntness in the way men, particularly, move across space, confront each other, or communicate by voice or hands or looks. Some might describe this absence of restraint as Slavic or more negatively as patriarchal. Others denote it as abruptness, straightforwardness, rudeness, or simply honesty. Yet these words don't capture a behaviour or ontology patently different from the one hundred kilometres north in Austria or from the prim Anglo-Saxon dominant still evident in parts of my nation. If there is a source for this aspect of the Croat character as it seems to exist in these moments, it may lie in the country, in some distant past, complicated by the passage of time.

As the tram continues towards Jelačić Square, the city begins to change. A brighter, denser regime of signs hangs in or outside store windows. The shops look like they offer things worth buying, or certainly more expensive ones than before. Near Jelačić

Square, the tram empties at a rate commensurate with the increase in shopping opportunities.

This Zagreb is transformed. Tall nineteenth-century Hapsburgian buildings are newly appointed in white, yellow, and cream. Entries and windows of shops are encased in marble and granite, and alleys and courtyards are lined by new shops, cafés, and fountains. More stylish young people swing through plane- and chestnut-treed boulevards as an air of civility and new affluence emerges. Yet Zagreb as I remember it has always been a cultured place, with its many museums, art galleries, book stores, music stores, and sophisticated intelligentsia. Everywhere in the centre are signs that the capital is site and symbol of the new Croatia, one belonging to that western and therefore "civilized" history merely interrupted by the Balkan Yugoslav experiment. Only Emil is sacrilegiously oblivious and continues to spray his name on the new façades.

I get out at the main square. About two football fields long and one wide, it's a palette of spring colours in the form of tall buildings ringing the space. Huge neon signs sit atop the roofs. A storey-high clock and a Christmas tree decorated with red bows stand on the western side of the square. It seems right to experience this new country and its new mood at a post-communist Christmas, symbolic time of birth and messianic promise.

Expressive of this mood is the bronze statue of nineteenth century Croatian military man and politician Josip Jelačić, who sits commandingly astride a horse on a chunk of granite. He used to point north towards Vienna and Budapest in seeming defiance of the Hungarians in the Austro-Hungarian Empire, though his position was actually determined by the Austrian architect's wish that Jelačić face the majority of Zagreb's population, not the horse's rear.[2] When the statue was returned to the square at the end of communist rule, it was turned to face south. Some Croats now say he raises his sword respectfully towards Dubrovnik, the naval trade bastion and literary heart of Renaissance Croatia. But most understand his position as a warning to Serb rebels in the former Vojna Krajina (military frontier, a buffer zone in south-central Croatia established by the Austrians in

1538 to repel Turkish advances, many of whose soldiers were Orthodox and whose descendants tried to secede from Croatia in 1990).

Josip Jelačić (1801–1859) was born near the Serb city of Novi Sad, in the Yugoslav province of Vojvodina. His military campaigns against the Turks on behalf of the Hapsburg Empire, which still ruled Croatia, and his popularity with his troops in the Vojna Krajina set him apart and marked him for political life. Chosen by the Illyrians, founders of a southern Slavic cultural movement begun in the 1830s to resist Hungarian nationalism, Jelačić accepted the post of *ban* (viceroy), officially conferred on him by the Croatian Sabor (assembly).

Jelačić swore an oath of allegiance to the Hapsburg emperor Ferdinand in Vienna, but not to Hungary. He was charged with treason and eventually ordered by Ferdinand, who had been swayed by the Hungarians, to report to Budapest. The workers' demonstrations in Vienna in 1848 fortuitously forestalled any charges, and Jelačić was formally instated as *ban* in an auspicious ceremony. He "rode into Zagreb on a white horse, dressed in the *ban*'s traditional costume of white, red and silver with eagle plumes in his hat. The welcome that he received was magnificent. Cannons thundered and church bells rang the whole day while in the evening there was an open-air feast and a firework display."[3]

Jelačić and other Croats expected Croatia would achieve a form of independent nationhood under the loose but protective auspices of the Austrian Empire. National sentiment, "exasperated by the incipient Magyar tyranny, had rallied round the throne of Habsburg. There was no other way out ... In turning to the Emperor, the people believed it was turning to a protector, and going to find peaceful haven for its national aspirations."[4] They were disappointed. Austria's new government rewarded them by ignoring their wishes.

Jelačić's resistance to Hungary has been alternately savaged by the communists as the slavish bootlicking of Austrian feet and praised by Croat nationalists as the heroic defence of their historic rights. Post-World War Two Yugoslav ruler Josip Broz (Tito, 1893–1980) renamed the square Republic Square and had the statue boarded up within a structure celebrating women against fascism—then secretly had it dismantled one night because he was concerned about rising Croat nationalist sentiments on the centenary of the rebellions of 1848. The statue remained in the basement of the Gliptoteka Gallery until Yugoslavia's first death throes in 1990. It was put back together again and the square renamed after Jelačić.

Such gestures show the part signs and symbols play in the semiotics of Croat and Yugoslav nationalism, which are as heavy with importance as those anywhere else in the world. Tito's renaming of Zagreb's other streets and squares, like nearby Trg Bratsva i Jedinstva (Brotherhood and Unity Square), was an attempt to enforce the reality of his rule on the minds of an unconverted public—as if only language were needed. But like the territorial spray of a dog, these names didn't last forever. Besides, the meaning of places is often determined by local history rather than official decree. Brotherhood and Unity Square was known as Flower Square because of its long identity as a market selling fresh flowers and dried bouquets for important moments in people's lives: deaths, marriages, and births. Now people once again joke that they will meet *pod repom* (under the tail).

The spirit of this post-communist Zagreb drew the Croat diaspora back, yet it was from Zagreb that many escaped after World War Two. My father was one of these. In 1964, just nineteen years old, he and a friend sneaked into the city's railway yard and onto a train that took them to their new lives.

Abandoned by his mother when he was two, so poor growing up that he shared a pair of rubber boots with his brother on the way to school in the winter, my father's beginnings weren't promising. And while he only had two weeks' salary from his job as a machine-fitter, he had the courage to get out of Yugoslavia. Using a universal key borrowed from a rail worker, my father and his friend entered a Paris-bound compartment one night, detached the ceiling, and had another friend bolt them back in. Twenty-three hours later they smashed their way out. Their two weeks' pay was enough for a night's stay in a hotel. Instead, they headed straight for the Eiffel Tower and slept in some bushes.

I tell his story briefly, not because it says something about his character or even explains how I came to be (how he made it to Vancouver, tried to sweet-talk my mother on Sunset Beach, etc.) but because it's also about the relationship between country and city. Zagreb at that time was the portal through which my father and others left behind their country roots (and a political system) in chasing the dream of a better life. Now the better life appears to have come here.

As I pass by the station, shoppers stream out of the massive underground Importanne Centar. In this part of town, I'm not able to access any images from the world my father left behind; rather, I find myself either in the present or, because of the style of the buildings and promenades, in nineteenth-century Austria. The intervening years seem to have been elided like a bad memory, my journey across Zagreb analogous with the way citizens view history itself. Indeed, changes to the old core seem like an objectification of a long-standing desire to belong in the west, even if the form this desire now takes is essentially materialistic. In finally arriving here, the dream of my father's seems to have been pared down to a posh landscape of boutiques in which most people can't shop.

Although my father escaped a three-year army stint as well as a lifetime of low wages, most Croats stayed on. The people I knew while I was growing up generally worked hard, even for low wages. Yet despite the heralded arrival of capitalism, which promised a better future, there is evidence that not everything is well. There are beggars, after all. Not normally worth noting in a city of nearly a million people, few beggars ever existed here, and their presence signals a rip in the social fabric.

The first I see today is an older man with a dough face peppered by blackheads; a pale stump sticks out of his grimy brown pants. He's sitting outside the entrance of the former Yugo-owned department store called NAMA (short for Narodni Magazin, the people's store). His sign claims that he's a veteran of the Vukovar siege in eastern Slavonia and can't find work. No one seems to believe him because his cardboard box is still empty when I return an hour later. Veterans of the war are honoured and have usually landed decent pensions, so it's more likely that his old-age security doesn't support him adequately in the city. These days it's better to be an old peasant than an old urbanite.

The second beggar is an eight- or nine-year-old Gypsy kid sitting cross-legged near Zagreb's new McDonald's off Jelačić Square. While his kind have been around Zagreb before now, they are more prevalent than ever. This kid is barefoot and is sticking his right hand out at the people going by. I stop a woman who is carrying two Donna Karan bags and ask her about the boy.

"No one ever loved Gypsies," she tells me. "His parents send him down here to earn their wages. I see them all the time. Spreading disease, aaahhh..." she trails off angrily. Although Croats elsewhere in the country might agree with her about Gypsies, they would probably label her *Purger*, the pejorative term for the snobbish Zagreb urbanite, derived from the "burghers" of the city's Hapsburgian past. *Purger* attitudes have hardened against what the intelligentsia call the ruralization of Zagreb—the inundation of refugees from rural parts of Croatia and Bosnia-Herzegovina since the war. These "carpet-baggers" speak their own dialects, are said to climb the social ladder aggressively, and stick together ferociously. They are mocked by urbanites with the all-purpose denigration *seljaci* (peasants).

On the bottom of the social ladder, below peasants, are Gypsies. In Sveta Nedjelja county where my father was born, I used to hear Gypsies before I saw them. They would call out to advertise their goods, and peasants would run in from the fields to lock their houses. Then came the sound of bells on the horses' bridles, the clop of hooves, and the Gypsies themselves on wooden wagons, the wagons piled with wicker baskets, copper pots, curtains, hand cloths, towels, and kerchiefs. I recall Gypsy women from my boyhood who looked much like the stereotypical images I came across later; they had bundles on their backs and wore old blouses and skirts, wildly coloured kerchiefs tied behind at the nape of their necks, gold earrings, necklaces, bracelets, and rings on every finger. That's where they seemed to carry their wealth. They were pushy vendors who tenaciously pursued a sale because they were poor.

Years later, I met a very different-looking Gypsy woman begging for money and food in a village south of Zagreb. She'd made an effort to appear proper and middle class. Her short hair wasn't bound in a kerchief; she wore a white blouse buttoned at the neck, a plain polyester skirt, and plastic sandals. But the kid hanging off her hand was barefoot, had matted hair and a face caked with dirt, and wore a jam-sticky Mickey Mouse shirt and yellow underwear. The woman insisted on unfolding a frayed document to prove that she was a widow (her husband had died in the war). We gave her some bread and roast pork off our barbecue. Even when she broke from her politeness to swear viciously at another of her kids in the road, who'd been calling her to leave, she convinced me of the basic truth of her performance.

I learned from these encounters that Gypsy life hasn't entirely changed, but that it has taken on new forms. While Gypsies occasionally camp under the bridge in Strmec, not far from the area I returned to year after year, I haven't seen a caravan since my boyhood. I doubt that this child knows his ancestors' way of life, but he has the same tenacity. The second I stop to look at him, he's all over me, so in exchange for a photo I buy him an order of fries at McDonald's. Before I leave, he asks me for more money. Although I refuse, I later remember people's assumption that such kids probably await a beating at home should they come back empty-handed.

Old Zagreb, or Agram as it was called in German, is a stone maze north of Jelačić Square and was once riven into two violently feuding towns during the Middle Ages. Krvavi Most (Bloody Bridge) spanned the stream that divided Kaptol, an archbishopric established in the eleventh century and inhabited by church officials and clerks, from Gradec to the southeast, once the nobility's fortified haven shared with lay citizens. The arguments had to do with property jurisdiction issues, like who had control over the mills.

A contributing factor to the division between clerical and lay classes was King Bela IV of Hungary's decision to confer on Gradec and other large towns the status of royal free cities. He sought to embolden trade and undermine the growing might of feudal lords following the crown's loss of authority throughout Croatia because of the Mongol invasions (from which he had found haven for a time in Gradec before escaping to the Adriatic coast). The year was 1242 and a massive Mongol army was razing the countryside, inflicting heavy defeats wherever it went, including Bela's army on the Sajo River. But according to one zealous historian, it was the Croats who saved Europe from one of the greatest dangers in its history: "in Croatia, this army experienced its first losses on the way from Peking to the Adriatic. In spite of a long siege, Batu Khan was not able to break the defense of the fortress of Kalnik (northern Croatia), where King Bela had taken refuge."[5]

Three hundred years passed, and then the Church murdered Matija Gubec and showed that at least the peasants could be controlled. Gubec was a serf from Zagorje who started a rebellion in 1573 over the seriously deteriorated living standards of his people. Ottoman incursions into Croatia led to perpetual fighting for the feudal estates, which were run by nobles and church officials who owned thousands of serfs. The dictatorial Bishop of Zagreb and *ban* of Croatia, Juraj Drašković, who sought to entrench the feudal system and prevent the Krajina example where Orthodox peasants had been freed in exchange for military service, had Gubec dragged to Sveti Marko church in the Gradec quarter and crowned with molten iron. As one historian put it, he was "crowned with a white-hot iron cow muzzle to symbolize a peasant king and seated upon a white-hot iron harrow as upon a peasant throne."[6]

Under a pretty snowfall, I arrive at Sveti Marko to see the spot where Gubec perished. A parking lot for ministers of the Sabor is half empty beside it. Huddling in small groups are some young *policija*, the only sign of authority today. There's a cozy medieval feeling here, and the church seems too humble to have an air of merciless ecclesiastical power. Built originally in the thirteenth century and inlaid on the roof with tile emblems of Croatia, Dalmatia, Slavonia, and Zagreb, it is simpler and more Slavic-looking than the buildings at the square. It has become a symbol of nationalist as much as ecclesiastical importance.

However, the intersection of church and state has found its real focus in a different church nearby. As seems to have become requisite for foreign writers, I visit Sveti Stjepan (St. Stephen) cathedral to see the tomb of a Croat saint—presumably a more just religious authority than Juraj Drašković. The marble relief of Alojzije Stepinac (1898–1960) by Croat sculptor Ivan Meštrović is almost naïve in its simplicity. Jesus Christ stands before the kneeling and praying former Archbishop of Zagreb, blessing him, His right hand horizontal over and behind the raised head, palm outward facing the viewer.

Meštrović made the point that Stepinac's relationship with Christ ultimately remained intact, but the Archbishop's supplicatory position makes him appear guilty of something. Herein lies the essence of the

Stepinac's tomb in Sveti Stjepan cathedral (Zagreb).

man himself, a man of God who seemed to need absolution but who insisted at his trial in Yugoslavia after the war, "my conscience is clear." Stepinac was Archbishop during Croatia's Nazi puppet dictatorship, and he compromised his integrity forever by publicly endorsing it in this church on Easter Sunday 1941. His reported dislike for Orthodox Serbs spurred his involvement, yet it became clear to him as time wore on that the new government was genocidal. In letters to Ustaša leader Ante Pavelić, he condemned the violence; he began working behind the scenes to save Serbs, Jews, and persecuted Catholics, and he delivered sermons about racial and ethnic tolerance. But in some ways he didn't change, remaining a staunch anti-communist and Croat nationalist until the end.

Writers have devoted considerable attention to the legacy of Stepinac. Some writers have reductively conveyed the country's essence as an unresolved relationship with its Ustaša past through one man. As a gesture to journalistic balance, I record the words of a nun walking up Bakačeva Ulica towards the cathedral. Her face freezes when I mention Stepinac in the same sentence as the Ustaše. "He was a good man, certainly. He lived in a difficult time, but he always followed his heart." Even in support of Stepinac, her words sound ambiguous. Aside from sounding wary, her voice seems tired when she discusses him. She's saying Croatia should be absolved from guilt for events so long ago, an absolution that would have occurred more quickly had Yugoslavia not disintegrated and the shadows of extreme nationalism not returned.

Tito also may have doubted Stepinac's guilt, although perhaps he was just politically shrewd. After the Archbishop's refusal to separate the Croatian Church from Rome, Tito sentenced him to sixteen years of imprisonment in Lepoglava, where he himself served time, but released him after five years and allowed his burial in the modern shrine of Catholic Croatia. Stepinac was beatified by Pope John Paul II in 1998.

I don't expect to meet any saints among the vendors at Dolac, Zagreb's sprawling market north of Jelačić Square, as I don't in any other market in the world. The woman who tries to sell me a brand-new cotton jersey from the stack on her table, claiming they are all seventy years old, makes me wonder if she would have tried this ruse on a local (i.e., someone without an accent).

Dolac is crammed this Saturday morning. Tarpaulins steamily shade narrow aisles between stalls, as people crab-walk by each other and hunker over the offerings and vendors weigh produce in brown paper bags on old weigh scales and shout out prices. Folk music cheerfully jingles from somewhere, mixed with the thud of dance pop from cafés. Along the outside ring of stalls are a few dealers in folk items: wooden bowls, plates, and vases engraved with the signature Croat design—the checkerboard *šahovnica*—or engraved with grapes, zigzag lines, or geometrical shapes. There are wood mosaics of Zagreb scenes like Sveti Marko church or the Kamenita Vrata (Stone Door) of the old town, where hundreds of candles in the archway are lit every day by parishioners, and there's kitsch like car doilies, stickers, flags, and shot glasses, all bearing the inescapable red and white checks.

The old spirit of Dolac is gone. On market Sundays as recently as the first half of the twentieth century, peasants used to show up with live chickens in cages, meat hanging in wagons, and other produce transported in baskets on their heads. Women wore pleated white cotton dresses, white sashes or aprons tied around their waists, shawls over their shoulders, bodices of flowery lace, and kerchiefs tied forward like hoods. The men wore round or flat-topped bowler hats, loose thigh-length shirts closed with slack bow ties, beaded vests, and baggy trousers.

Only a few peasants, mostly women, now occupy the fruit and vegetable stalls on the upper level of this market. The peasant vendors are characterized by the humble piles of in-season produce grown on their own land. Vendors standing behind mountains of Slavonian beets and other vegetables are often non-farming entrepreneurs who truck produce in and sell it at higher prices.

Under Dolac, in the enclosed section that houses butcher shops and bakeries, peasant women still sell homemade cheeses and sour cream. They no longer wear their colourful folk clothing. Fewer of these women come than before because many are too old, while others don't find it worth their while or have found customers closer to home, such as the "weekenders" from Zagreb. Ultimately, there are fewer peasants, especially in larger urban centres.

This waning of the peasantry isn't a brand-new phenomenon, but one that has intensified in recent years. For me this reality has been registered, indirectly, in nostalgic art. Ironically, the city is a main site for art about peasants. Zagreb's galleries and museums are full of paintings by Croatia's naïve school, the Zemlja (land or earth) group. Perhaps the best-known member is Ivan Generalić (1914–1992), who turned out a considerable corpus of peasant-based work that could deflect accusations of being patronizing because of his country origins.

Although these "primitive" works might express an innocent rural sensibility, they can never really escape the childish ways in which the people depicted in them appear to think—what comes across as their entire *gestalt*. One painting, for example, shows a peasant woman sitting on a wooden stool in the snow as a small, pinkish horse with thick, childishly drawn hooves moves towards her. Her mouth is open as if she's talking to the animal. Through this gentle connection between human and animal (or pet), the painting decisively enters the naïve since it abandons the usual reality of peasant–animal relations: the fact that domesticated animals serve a purely functional purpose in sustaining human lives. In such a painting, the world as it is becomes the world as it might be.

This utopian purpose is perhaps more evident in later naïve works through the use of brighter colours (painted on glass), which makes the paintings more naïve yet, paradoxically, more sophisticated. The bright colours seem like symbolic compensation for peasant drudgery. Scenes of village life show enormous flowers, birds the size of cows, spring-green grass, and blooming plants juxtaposed with spectral trees in fall, gaudy skies like those in paintings sold at malls, and happy, puppet-like peasants at work or rest, often wearing yellow or orange *nošnje* (heavy cotton clothing). These dreamscapes also seem to represent a surrealistic longing on the painters' part for a past that no longer exists, or never did. The Croat peasants I know don't dream of their world in this manner. They generally accept the reality of their lives and instead find different outlets as compensation, like small pleasures and ceremonies.

If there's one thing I'm searching for as I leave Zagreb for rural Prigorje, it's the actual state of the peasantry, so long a cornerstone of northern Croat life. In Prigorje I expect to see few signs of the psychology and ambiance of the capital, the country's military fulcrum,[7] site of the Sabor, of political rule and contestation, of the media's main circuits, if only because peasants have placed the pressing concerns of land higher on their hierarchy of values, are maybe more skeptical about the vanities of power when they have to negotiate each day with the earth.

3  PRIGORJE
The Good Air

OUTSIDE ZAGREB LIE THE FLATLANDS AND HILLS of Prigorje where I've returned year after year like some proverbial wandering Jew looking for a home. For me, the spiritual centre of Prigorje (which literally means "by the hills") is a piece of land in the hamlet of Srebrnjak, twenty kilometres south of the city. On this spot stood the peasant dwelling where my father was born. Here live Štefek and Mila Juranko, the couple who helped raise him in place of his real parents.

In the summer, Srebrnjak is a lush valley with fruit orchards, cornfields, and dense vegetation. Now, in the winter, it's brown and spectral. At the mouth of the valley is a grey wooden crucifix under a little roof covered by snow. Farmhouses strung one after another along the road send up lines of pale smoke. Old wooden barns, yards dotted with chickens, and big mangy dogs sticking their heads out of their houses complete the medieval picture. In the fields stand dark trees, their branches spiking the cold sky, and filigrees of ice-sheathed brambles adorn the side of the road in bright clusters. At one time, the houses here were two-room wooden ones, but now they're two storeys tall, mostly built out of orange bricks or blocks, usually façaded by white plaster and topped with orange tiles.

Štefek and Mila are the last farmers on the Srebrnjak road. Further up are a few abandoned farmhouses among the overgrowing trees— outhouses and barn roofs sagging and covered by moss. Some forgotten vineyards in the higher reaches of the valley and grassy undulations hinting at former roads once destined for the still primitive and tiny Lacković Breg are all that's left of farmers' labour here. On such former roads, my father lazily herded cows for Štefek, and from up here, turkeys became airborne when they were chased back home. The old ways are dying and gradually the lives and architecture of weekenders will take over Srebrnjak.

Štefek's barn is a long structure of concrete and dark stained wood. Smoke rises steadily from a rusty tin chimney. Plum branches stick up over the roof, and way up on the hill two square vineyards, their poles lined up like sentinels, wait patiently for the summer sun. Dried, still-fragrant hay fills the loft, and braided onions hang from a beam with some scythes, sickles, and rope. The room is small and dark and filled with the aroma of cooking plums. On this quiet winter afternoon, Štefek is going to distill a few litres of *šljivovica* (plum brandy). And I'll be the first to taste it.

An old contraption against the far concrete wall, the still is a copper assembly of tubs and narrow pipes hooked up to a black wood stove slitted by air vents. It has the look of some junk trucked here and put together, but it works well enough, clear drops falling steadily into a white pail. Štefek is sitting beside the still like a parishioner in front of an altar. He's got on a grey cap slanted over his eyes, a brown suit jacket buttoned tightly over layers of tatty work sweaters, brown pants from the same suit (a throwback to the archaic loose breeches he wore as a boy), and scuffed black workboots that look two sizes too big for him. Hanging on a nail is his blue work jacket from his days twenty years ago at a lead and aluminum factory—the Yugoslav workers' colour he wears now and again out of habit instead of nostalgia. Even in this half-light I recognize his sharp blue eyes, eagle's nose, and those high Slavic cheekbones. It's a face that can pin you with a look but smile gently too. "So you're here," he says.

"Here I am," I answer. "Look at that, you already have half a litre."

"Not to drink yet," he says. "It's almost pure alcohol."

I remember being offered this form of *šljivovica* one summer from a guy over the hill in Dol. His head was oily and his soiled white shirt stuck to his belly. His growly voice slurred words at me. "Here, just a little stronger than rainwater." I was more of a romantic then and wanted to participate in "old country" experiences but the *šljivovica* wasn't recognizable and burned my throat. I told him it was pretty good. A neighbour who was there tried to shame the guy—but carefully because it wasn't his own place.

There's no evil here today. Štefek and I sit on a bench, silently watching the brandy drip into the pail. He sticks some wood into the stove and the fire spits and crackles, then hums again, flickering light around the room. Now that there's nothing to do, he seems at a loss; his thick hands have fallen awkwardly in his lap as if they'd ended up in a foreign place. This posture of inaction belongs to people who do manual work all their lives and equate leisure with laziness. Old people spend their last winter days close to their stoves, feeling guilty, their empty hands open with the palms up like beggars seeking alms.

But something about distilling *šljivovica* in the slow time of the year makes inaction different. Štefek behaves differently: he is relaxed, maybe even bored. *šljivovica* itself doesn't interest or motivate him because he stopped drinking twenty years ago.

"Why do you bother if you never drink it?" I ask him.

"What would I do with all these plums?"

"You could eat them. Mila could bake pies."

He thinks about my words for a moment. "I don't like plums," he says. Habit and tradition are hard to shake out of people here, probably because lives connected to the soil are inherently repetitive— the cycle of seasons, the repetition of tasks and actions. His father and grandfather before him made *šljivovica*, so he does too.

Something unarticulated hides inside Štefek, traceable in the simple elements of the event itself: the smell and sound of the fire, a warm cocooning darkness on a cold day. The unspoken feeling is the pleasure of this familiar ceremony that ties him to this place. Distilling *šljivovica* is the closest he will ever come to having a hobby, embarrassing as this might be for him. Leisure for Štefek is always connected in some way to the land, which is also the source of his labour. And while he might gripe about his work or about the weather, any fundamental change to his life would be impossible, counter-intuitive; this life is all he knows, all he imagines for himself, because he doesn't dream.

After watching the pail fill up for a while, I follow him to the barn where he has some chores. Thick wet flakes are spiralling down, arriving like a beautiful gift so close to Christmas. The spaces between them and their trajectories seem synchronized as if by design, and I watch them appreciatively. They might presage some goodness to come, or maybe they point no further than themselves, carrying that magical charge of happiness with their own arrival.

The snow doesn't have any effect on Štefek; after all, when else should snow fall except in the winter? He's shouting at his two cows and whipping one of them on its backside for sitting in its own mess. A tirade of abuse pours from him, perfunctory really, like another habit in his day, and only superficially comparable to the patriarchal bluntness I'd observed in Zagreb and Pag. Pitchforking the cow-pie and dirty straw out a small back door, he orders Beba towards the wall. Every cow I've seen in this stall has been named Beba and every cow near the door has been Maca. They're usually chained here when they're calves and freed when they die. In between, they never leave. Of course, neither does Štefek Juranko.

Waiting for the brandy to be ready, I climb to the top of the hill and take in the view. On clear days, Zagreb shines white in the distance, the twin spires of the cathedral clearly visible. Today there is only the haze of falling snow through which even the nearby houses and the road below are hardly visible. Clearer to the southwest, waves of hills and valleys recede to the horizon as if too much land were jammed in the allotted space between here and the Adriatic Sea. Indeed, I feel that these hills will never end, so even and constant is their progression.

I'm not alone in experiencing this illusion of endless continuity. Art critic and novelist John Berger writes that this illusion, which he experienced in Serbia, exists not only because of the light in the sky or the colour of the hills produced by distance, but because "no event in the landscape (no hill, no tree, no building) is so striking that it

Wooden crucifix, now replaced, at the entrance of Srebrnjak (Prigorje), 1997.

creates a natural focal centre to which everything else becomes subservient."[1]

Standing on this hill in my childhood, I would have agreed. Then, the Marija Magdalena chapel, perched on the highest point here, had long been assimilated into the world around it: the façade had fallen to pieces, revealing grey-brown stone the colour of the clayish earth; trees and bushes had suffocated it so that, from certain places in the valley, the chapel was completely hidden. It had regressed to the state of a natural object so old and familiar it went unnoticed.

But Marija Magdalena has been refurbished and painted a golden Hapsburgian yellow that is still evident throughout Zagreb and northern Croatian towns. The chapel seems to have left the "primitive" Slavic world for the "civilized" Austrian one, or maybe it reclaimed its Catholic identity, which had languished over time. Now the chapel itself is that event to which everything else becomes subservient. For visitors who haven't lived all their lives in this valley, it's a sign of another age, to which their eyes are inevitably drawn. The ideal intention of the chapel's builders was to guide each viewer from an arresting sight towards an equally strong awareness of God's presence.

Marija Magdalena is mainly a silent, unused place except on certain occasions like its name's day every July 22, when people from all around stream to the top in their Sunday best. Then vendors from the area set up kiosks, selling kids' toys and religious doilies, strings of pink candied cookies and glasses of dark, sweet *gverc* (like mead). The smell of barbecuing pork rises into the sky. Somewhat separate, as if in deference to the day but still part of the festivities, are crowds of smoking, drinking men around tubs of iced beer and wine. Once the service is over and the people who could fit inside spill into the yard, the *tamburica* music begins—happy balalaika-ish orchestras accompanied by cheerful voices.

Once a year, Marija Magdalena is site of a gaudy celebration with just enough signs of the old world—in the form of priests and choir-boys and old people in their kerchiefs and felt hats and canes—to save it from being a purely commercial event. From the perspective of this winter day so far removed in time and season, snow spiralling down and whitening the brown country, July 22 is hard to imagine. As I cross the top of the hill, bands of sparrows swoop from skeletal tree to tree in fluid, amoebal formations and the silence suddenly drops on my mind like a sound and I stop to listen.

I step out of a lane of trees and shrubs into a little amphitheatre surrounded by big oaks. Marija Magdalena is more imposing than I remember it; a view from a faraway hill only gives it the quality of a decoration atop a Christmas tree. The chapel seems to soar upwards into the sky's grey ceiling. But the wood door is small and the entrance so low that I would have to duck my head to get in.

Just as I'm going to turn away, I notice two small initials carved into the door. They are my own and someone else's. No thought or image or memory comes to me at first, but then suddenly I remember. I'm back ten years ago when I came here with a girl from Brezje, a moment returning to me like some fossil discovered accidentally. From that late summer walk I remember her curly hair, a shade lighter than caramel; her whispering voice, musical, cadenced; and the mystery of her presence, which has stayed with me all this time. We walked through the tall grass along the top of the hill holding hands some of the way. She told me her grandmother had just died and that I was saving her.

Marija Magdalena chapel (Prigorje), 1997.

We went inside the chapel—in those days the door was unlocked and creaked easily open—and said some brief nuptial vows though we hardly knew each other. On another day with someone else, our musty voices might have sniggered spookily, but instead they echoed in a cozy, hollow, timeless way, the way it is inside an old stone building in an old country when you're young—or in love.

Štefek dips the shot glass into the nearly full pail and hands it to me, saying, "Now it won't poison you." The clear liquid doesn't quite scald my throat, but it heats up my chest and then my head soon after.

"Warm," I mutter. "Good." A faint plum taste lingers somewhere in my throat, weakened but refined through distillation. The pleasure of this brandy for me isn't just the taste or the effect on my system but also the recognition of that line from source to final product, from the trees that blossom in the spring and mature in the heat and finally blanket the ground or plastic sheets with plums, after some shaking, to the barrels where the plums ferment and finally burn through copper tanks and pipes and purify into the drops that fill this pail. There's also a trace of human energy along this circuit: not just the sun and rain or the flow inside the veins of trees, but Štefek's labour, which is the connector, the propulsion from step to step, yet not traceable the way brushstrokes on their canvases speak of painters' hands.

"So, Štefek," I ask, "will you try your new brew?" He looks at me like he's considering it, then answers, "You just drink." He shows no signs of really wanting to himself, no regret for the old days, if there were any, when he freely drank his own stuff or his father's before that—not just brandy but also the sour, earthy white wine from these hills, stored in big wooden barrels in their dank dark cellars, a wooden or plastic faucet sticking from one and a wicker or glass demijohn waiting expectantly underneath. Hanging from the walls or ceilings were knives and sausages and half moons of cheese in their stockings.

I can't imagine Štefek roaming Zagreb at night with other young guys and carousing messily until all hours. But I do see him in one of these rooms, either alone or with his father or brother, or at the head of a family dinner table drinking and talking politics—a kind of patriarch comfortable in his position, no longer watching with any expectation or interest the reactions of his in-laws to the food and drink that he and his wife provided. Instead, his unspoken satisfaction with the structure, the correctness of those moments, emanated from him, as if a higher hand arranged them and he had nothing really to do with it. Always, though, Štefek's relationship with liquor is tidy and clean, not sloppy or brutal, as if it had always a place in his set of values and was understood and tempered. Now every year, he concentrates the work of summer and fall—and sixty-odd years of memories—into these hours, into the containers in his cellar.

With a buzz in my head, I start back down the Srebrnjak road for a walk. It's late in the afternoon now and getting dark. The country

Gathering last summer's corn stalks (Prigorje), 1997.

and the houses themselves seem to be settling in for the night. The dogs are quiet and snow falls only intermittently; the distance between flakes is wider like the gap between myself and Štefek's house, the new night and old day.

At the end of the road, I stop by the crucifix and look up the valley at the church shrouded by dusk. In the hills, night seems to have already fallen, but here, because of the streetlight nearby, the crucifix is still clear. If Jesus ever imagined a meeting between Himself and others in some far corner of the world, some momentary but powerful connection, a sharing or understanding of suffering across the centuries, it would be in a place like this. Here, on foot, it's possible above all to stop and consider His image, to consent to time and think about its meaning, though such a moment is rare and tenuous sometimes, even the click of my camera cutting me off.

In this dying agrarian world, the two poles of life outside of work are faith and liquor—Marija Magdalena and *šljivovica*. Divided by gender, these poles are too distant to be bridged, even if their "apparatuses"—altar and still—and their final results aren't totally dissimilar. But while one aims upwards at the scoured and bright stars, the other is bound always to the ground, the earth now quiet and cold but rich long enough each summer to produce a testimony to itself.

■

After every Christmas, parish priests trudge through the villages ringing a bell, singing in front of doors, prayer books in hand, looking tired and defeated.[2] Kids are usually out around the same time of year, blowing tin cans sky-high with a carbide derivative instead of firecrackers. On New Year's Eve, men band at crossroads with shotguns and pistols—young punks and middle-aged greaseheads in Fortrel sweaters and leather bomber jackets that don't close around their bellies anymore, swaggering and joking and shouting with cigarettes clamped between their teeth, swigging beers and mickeys of brandy, shooting out the stars. They're all ringing in the new year, but only the priests are solemn about it.

The holy water comes from the tap at the church in Sveta Nedjelja but is blessed by the priest. The most devout await his visit with a filled glass and a wand of spruce, which he dips in the water and sprinkles around to bless the house for the new year. Very often there's another glass, a glass of wine (for "replenishment"). The less devout don't bother with the water and the wand but still open their doors to him and his chaplain, and for these cases he brings holy water of his own. A few lock their doors and turn out the lights.

During these visits, everyone knows the operating dynamic. It's understood that the priest, who's so "replenished" sometimes that he has difficulty performing his duties, accepts donations to the church. Once people invite him in, they feel obliged to offer a sum, an offering to God's presence in their homes. Sometimes this is more than they can afford. It's understood that the priest never asks but never refuses either—not even the oldest and the destitute, who often happen to be the most superstitious as well and can't take a chance that worse will happen this year.

Tito grew up in the neighbouring region of Zagorje in the late nineteenth century, but his memory of such events shows how some things haven't changed all that much. In his quasi-autobiographical book *Tito Speaks*, he recalls friars appearing after Christmas, "carrying a cross and followed by a sexton with a sack. A friar would chalk the words *Anno Domini...* on the door, thus wishing us a happy New Year, and the host would have to give him a few pounds of corn, a bunch of golden flax or two florints, which in those days meant two days' wages. You can imagine how we children felt as we stood by, hungry as usual, and watched the sexton pour our corn into his sack."[3]

People around Sveta Nedjelja suspect some priests of lining their own pockets with monetary contributions. When their residence was broken into in the late 1980s and all the money stolen, the official story went that thieves were responsible each time. Said the founder of the Croatian Peasants Party, Stjepan Radić, "One believes in God, but one judges the priest."

Malogorička Road winds below the hills south of Zagreb like a belt pulled from its loop holes and tossed among rumpled clothes. After a bike ride, I'm returning to Srebrnjak to load some hay. The sun is well up this June morning and big, wild, wolfish dogs behind their iron gates are howling at me, driving me on. In the daylight, their hysterical ferocity is laughable, but at night on badly lit roads with gates half open, they sound genuinely dangerous, their chains rattling on wires attached between houses and barns, hissing metal, jangling. And when one dog starts up, others bark wildly too so that my many trips from one neighbour to another were traced by these alarms, and people already half asleep knew that someone is out there, a traveller on the loose. But all the other competing sounds of the day make me mostly undetected this time.

Eventually I drive to the top of a hill that forms the northern side of Srebrnjak's U-shaped valley. The road, made of gravel and rocks and splintered brick, eventually becomes two tracks of sun-baked mud through tall grass and encroaching bushes. Crickets are singing in the fields, and bees are droning in the bowers of branches and brambles. A brown hawk performs an elegant turn, stately, buzzard-like. The view from above shows the road winding into the sun-hazed distance: pocket-sized houses and tiny farmers working on brown fields, only now sprouting belt-high corn and green wheat.

The riotous poverty of Lacković Breg sprawls on top of the western end of Srebrnjak, straight ahead were I to keep walking—unfaçaded houses crammed together claustrophobically as if the Lackovići knew fifty years ago that no one was ever going to leave and that they would eventually run out of space. There are mud- and shit-covered yards, mangy foaming dogs and rooting pigs, rotting clapboard hen-houses on stilts, rusting Yugo and Fiat carcasses already sinking into the ground, old people squatting on wooden stools or concrete steps or peering hollow-eyed from their windows, dirty kids scurrying like mice in and out of the streets; and, like the past that hasn't been forgotten yet, pleasantly idyllic in comparison and falling back into nature, empty nineteenth-century wooden dwellings, moss-tufted, filled with dove and chicken droppings. Štefek's is a more civilized world, with green spaces and fresh air. Chickens and turkeys are wandering around the grass yard and in the plum and apple orchards behind the barn.

A tiny man high on the hill behind the house is scything grass. Because the sound doesn't travel this far, the swaths cut by the strained but still elegant orbit of his arm fall behind as if by magic; the green waves look freed when they're cut, released, but they also look like the life has gone out of them. Now and again he stops and I know, though I can't see him clearly, that he's sharpening his blade on his whetstone. He pulls it from a tin holder on his belt and shakes the water off. The square he's working on is almost finished, and the one left of him is a greyer shade of green, turned once and ready for the barn.

I go down the steep hill through the dry soil of a weedy cornfield and then a patch of tall grass uncut since spring. It's studded with daisies and buttercups and maybells, and is alive with bees and grey snakes. Finally I jump over the ditch and land on the paved road.

Inside the kitchen are a black-and-white TV and a white wood stove. A framed picture of the Virgin Mary hangs on one wall, a Saints' Days calendar on another, keeping track of occasions for big meals instead of veneration. Mila lumbers about, moving pots on the stove, checking the meat frying in the pan inside, and stoking the fire with wood from the box her mother, Slava, used to sit on during her last years. I have a picture of Mila when she was twenty-five years old. She was a strong, wiry woman with hollowed cheeks burned from

Mila Juranko outside her house in Srebrnjak (Prigorje), 1997.

summer work, eyes level and almost hard—a woman too far removed in time to be this Mila. Now she's twice the size; her big hams are flared under her blue skirt, and her hands are swollen and cracked. One day I ask her if she knows how to swim. "Sure," she shoots back. "Like a stone."

Although it's the wrong time of day and the wrong weather, I fill a tumbler of *šljivovica* and sit outside the kitchen in the hot shade. For the moment I feel at peace, as if I belong here. As a boy I first learned Croatian in this yard and first played soccer in the field in front of the house. I know these hills and bramble-covered trails as well as any living person. My past is homing me towards a future in Srebrnjak as strongly as anywhere in Canada. And yet there have been signs or admissions that I belong there, not here. In the summer of 1987, for example, I painted a red maple leaf on the water trough under the walnut tree. It was my way, I suppose, of letting everyone know where I came from, who I really was.

But I think of identity and home less in nationalistic terms than I used to, as if behind the flag I'd uncovered another self, and found it in a specific place. What makes a Canadian-born son of immigrants look back across the ocean for a place to belong? I can't claim any of the artistic pretensions of the modernists' exile ("to create my art I must go"). These were never my reasons for coming to Croatia, even this time (Croatia isn't a place in which to write but a subject of my writing). What I do know is that the comfort I feel here is more intuited than it is expressible in words, and that the identity and home I claim for myself is still ambiguous, still hasn't assumed a final form.

I sit in silence outside the house. The heat, the sun's glare off the sharp green grass, and the *šljivovica* itself put me in a vacant but sensitive state. Every sound separates around me like individual instruments isolated from a symphony: the mournful hooting of doves on the wind, the sibilant pine branches and tall grass, the crowing of roosters and barking of dogs somewhere down the road, the angry whir of a hand mower in some vineyard, the buzz of flies and bees in the grass or against the kitchen windows, the chugging of Marko's little yellow tractor transporting a barrel of insecticide to his vineyard, the slick hiss of an Audi heading up to a weekend house, the banging of pots inside, and Mila's mumbling chatter.

Out of this irregular pattern a louder sound suddenly starts, then ends just as quickly, as if beginning and cessation were one: the alarmed clucking of chickens followed by their quiet bolt across the yard. They end up huddling in little packs under trees or against the barn, some sitting on top of others to save space, their heads darting left and right. Mila comes out of the house and when she sees them, she looks up and points at something: "Up there. *Jastreb.*"

Hardly more visible than a dot, a hawk is riding the wind casually, not much of a threat so high. But for these chickens, its dark presence has floated over the yard like the shadow of a cloud. Ten years before, I heard another uproar of clucking coming from the fenced-in chicken yard; I remember Mila's mother, Slava, hurrying out of the kitchen with a stick she kept by the door to round up turkeys that had wandered near the road. She waved her stick at the tail that jumped over the wire fence, trailing this time only a few brown feathers.

Slava swore, grabbed the half-dead chicken by the shoulders, and dropped it outside the barn's big sliding doors, where it flopped around without a sound. She went into the tool room, then behind the barn where I couldn't see.

So it was, as far back as I can remember. The light was different then, colours Polaroid cheap, sounds missing. Flashes of such events are all I recall, like slides projected somewhere in the back of my head that I view intimately but as a stranger: Slava snatching a healthy bird, tucking it under her arm, her arm jerking back and white wings flapping, then, jarred out of my fascination, my running to the house, where the disturbing feeling went away.

Even five minutes after breezes drift the *jastreb* down the valley, the chickens still cower against each other. Mila and I move the kitchen table outside. She brings out a pot of beef bouillon, thick with two-inch-long noodles, and pours a bowl to cool for Štefek. Usually she calls him from work, but there's no need this time because he's already halfway down the hill, as if he smelled lunch wafting his way. Over his shoulder is his scythe; the blade swoops behind him like a scimitar and his squat shadow walks ahead of him.

The sun wasn't out the last time I saw him cresting the same hill out of a thick fog that still hadn't burned off in the late morning. By chance, I looked up from the road the second the faint outline of his head and arms and scythe emerged insect-like through the mist, slowly sharpening in outline into the form of a man, somewhat clearer now after he climbed the hill's nub through the last veils of fog. But at that moment, he wasn't a man at all; he was an archetype, a museum piece from some other time.

Štefek joins us after splashing his taut sunburned face in the kitchen sink and combing back his thin grey strands of hair, using the little mirror hanging from a nail inside the window. This is a gentlemanly sort of thing to do, and surprisingly vain.

Despite the pictures on the walls, no one ever bothered to say grace here except Slava, secretively and ashamedly because she didn't want to be laughed at. So we begin eating right away. The next course is the boiled beef with eye-watering *hren* or horseradish sauce prepared from the tough roots that grow in gardens everywhere here. Today's main meal consists of fried chicken; fries; *mlinci* noodles that were first baked on the stove-top, then cooked in the chicken pan; a salad of kidney beans dressed with oil, vinegar, and onions; and cornbread baked this morning. For dessert, there is freshly baked strudel filled with cherries from the tree out back, the one my father planted when he was a kid. This Sunday-type meal is for farmers who toil on the hill all day long. It's too rich and heavy for me, although not quite like it was ten years ago when Mila still cooked with pig fat, which had me running to the indoor toilet or outhouse, not knowing whether to sit or kneel. (The outhouse is still wedged between the pigsties and the barn, and is still used, even in the winter.)

Because work is their life, food is the fuel that keeps Štefek and Mila going. They eat a lot, their food hewn for bigger appetites than mine. Once in awhile, they relax after meals, on weekends or winter days when there's nothing to do, or in the summer when the heat stops the world for two hours every afternoon. But today they need to transport the grass to the barn, so they can't enjoy a slow meal.

Mila's menu has never really changed, dependent as it is on the seasons and on Štefek, a creature of habit who eats the same breakfast almost every day—*žganci* (cornmeal chunks) floating in milk and coffee. When my father barbecued steaks the way he'd learned it in Alberta, or boiled corn instead of baking it on embers inside the wood stove, Štefek and Mila watched him as if he were a circus animal performing tricks. They never tried a bite. It wasn't so much a choice as a way of life; it was as if they could do nothing else because they never learned to value anything new.

Like other farmers in Croatia, they're basically self-sufficient. All their labour has a place in a system; everything they grow, every kernel of corn, is used up to the end. They rarely have garbage to throw away. The wheat and corn they harvest provide feed for the pigs and chickens and turkeys, which in turn feed Štefek and Mila. The pork is cured and smoked into sausages in the attic, the fat cut into cubes, fried, and drained to make *čvarci*; intestines serve as sausage casings or are fed to the cats when the pigs are slaughtered (or were turned into bladders, in my father's boyhood, for homemade soccer balls).

Mila Juranko and pigs (Prigorje), 1997.

Leftover corn cobs fuel the stove in the upstairs bathroom. Residue at the bottom of wine barrels is distilled into *loza*. Shit from the outhouse and the barn fertilizes the land. And the cycle begins again.

Štefek's little tractor is a hip-high orange machine with a shiny chassis that gives it a car-show look. Even though he's had this tractor for years, he still handles it clumsily, as if it would always be a foreign or exotic piece of machinery, the shift a sort of wand that magically propels the vehicle forward and backward, surprising him every time it does. Mila and I hook up the wagon, two ladders joined in a V and a crank to brake the back axle, all riding on soft rubber tires.

We get a lift through the orchards along the undulating path to the top, where we turn sharply downhill and park alongside a long rectangular swath of cut grass. I hop off and turn the crank clockwise to lock the back wheel. We have two pitchforks and a wooden rake with wooden teeth for Mila, and we begin piling the grass in little ricks to load onto the wagon. My pitchfork is a shorter one for this kind of lifting work, thick and polished shiny from years of handling, like a stone lapped by water, the wood furrowed but showing no signs of coming apart. No longer young at seventy-four but fit enough to keep up with a fifty-year-old, Štefek spryly lifts himself onto the wagon and spreads out the grass I toss up. Obsessive when it comes to this work, he carefully and scientifically arranges the pile while Mila rakes every shred onto the ricks as if each blade were a rare golden ducat, leaving the hill looking like a stubbled jaw.

What's the meaning of this care, this entire operation, I wonder. After all, for the amount of milk and cheese they consume, and the little profit they make selling cheese to Zagreb weekenders, they probably only need one cow at the most.

"Štefek," I ask, "what's all this work for?"

He waits a second, his answer taking the form of another question. "Are you tired already?" I don't expect some practical and reasonable explanation, because I know the truth is less conscious for him and less justifiable, especially to someone from elsewhere—that custom is the real motor here. Do something long enough and it becomes life itself.

The wagon piled high and almost teetering, Štefek slides gingerly off the back end and ropes down the hay. On longer trips, a log is loaded on top and tied at both ends. As he drives the creaking, swaying wagon slowly down through the orchards and to the front of the barn, we follow with the tools over our shoulders. Now we sit at the table and wait. Their son-in-law will arrive later to help pile the hay in the loft; Mila's not strong enough to help Štefek and I'm too inexperienced. Lifting the tightly bound grass is no simple task; it demands deftness and moments of powerful leverage, bursts upwards that stress the lower hand and arm. In the meantime we rest and chat, watching the colours change.

The evening sun through the pine trees sends long menhir-like shadows over the shaven field in front of the house, halfway to Marko's property. His house is the same yellow as Marija Magdalena chapel, but it's smeared black under the upstairs window, as if dirty water has been tossed from there over the years. The house belongs to another time and not only because of its colour, but also its position in the surrounding space; there's a delicate balance here between a crowded

Štefek Juranko on a hay wagon (Prigorje), 1990.

assembly of objects on the one hand and openness on the other. Marko's place is bowered by plum, peach, cherry, and apple trees, as well as by four immense pines that were planted sixty years before by the old man. There is a hedge, once better cared for, running beside the road, along with the shabby architecture of chicken coops and wooden fences. Yet in the distance are little meadows, empty patches of fallow earth, and, like a bookend on the far side, hills fretted by vineyards and gardens and cornfields.

On the one hand, there's no way to escape humanity here—no plot of earth, no corner that hasn't been fashioned or trodden on, cultivated or harvested, so saturated is the earth with human action. On the other hand, as if in compensation, room enough for solitude or separation is arranged around the houses in the spaces between hilltops.

Ultimately, some barrier to vision lies in every direction so that no long sightline exists. This visual enclosure, not some psychological pressure from cage-like hills, is what ends up weighing on me after awhile, as if my eyes are trapped and need more space to roam. There's no illusion of limitless expanses for the eyes to travel nor the relief of nothing much to see, as in Canada, where in some places only the odd grain elevator or farmhouse gives a scene organization, or where strips of canola or wheat structure sights like bars of colour in an abstract painting. A lifetime of seeing in Srebrnjak changes thought itself; it sets borders on dreams and offers no distant horizon to make one wonder what's there or what adventure awaits.

The visual dilemma in Srebrnjak is neither unique nor comparable to the alienation felt going the other direction, where immense space intimidates the European consciousness. No one visiting Srebrnjak for the first time ever worries that nature will kill them. Knowing that everything in sight is also in reach, and that strangers with unknown names and pasts and motives rarely wander in, is probably comforting in some unconscious, unspoken way.

Haying in Srebrnjak is meaningful because it eliminates surprises and connects people to a familiar sequence of events belonging to this season, boring but comforting ceremonies of labour governed by the sun, the rain, and the earth.

■

Dead vineyards scrabble up the slopes on the upper reaches of Srebrnjak. Let nature run its course for even a year and the grapes will wither, grass and weeds start to choke the rows, and untended vines stray or break off the poles. Anemic grapes might survive a season but will die in two or three as hostile brambles and blackberries overgrow them. Around these graveyards are cracked benches and tables and rickety shacks (some still containing tools), where owners might have slept years ago with a shotgun to protect their harvests from thieves and kids like my father, who sneaked in to eat his fill. Those who tended these vineyards loved this work but either got too old to continue or died. Their vineyards went untended because their children weren't willing to devote long hours to the job.

New shacks are built on concrete, extended by concrete terraces for future rooms in little villas. Younger farmers and Zagreb week-enders use steel or concrete supports, tent mesh, and mowers instead of the traditional scythes. But some things go on unchanged. Owners still spray turquoise *galica* (an insecticide) on their vines through hoses hooked to tanks on their backs, like World War One flamethrowers. As part of an older way of life, these men still rest by their vineyards and drink and chaw over the next job. When they aren't alone, they begin that characteristic Croat dynamic centred on the most important piece of architecture—the table—across which they face each other as they chat, joke, work themselves up and unfurl one of their endlessly ongoing monologues about politics like a flag they wave in each other's faces, or deliver theories about winemaking, some minor technical imperative in farming, or timetables for smoking meat in the winter. They make arrangements for haying or borrowing machinery, or give expert advice about the national soccer team or economics (although not about making more money), or any number of other things while they fling their hands and slap the table. They stare across the valley when they stop listening and laugh "*ma da*" or "*ma kak*" (roughly, "like hell"), or swear to get out their anger in a manner more customary than immoral: "*odi u kurac*" (literally, "go to the cock") or "*pička ti materina*" (roughly, "your mother's cunt") or "*jebo ti pas mater*" ("may the dog fuck your mother") or "*jebem ti Boga*" ("I fuck your God") or "*Bog te jebo*" ("God fucks you") or "*Vrag te jebo*" ("the Devil fucks you") or "*Vrag te odnesel*" ("may the Devil take you away").

The picture was taken in 1977 and shows my father and me turning a wooden spit. The pig looks like it weighs fifty or sixty pounds, and has reached the golden brown that tells it's nearly done. In the background are plum trees, a hay rick, and our white 1969 Citroën DS Palas. This photo of father and son is rather idyllic, more so for what it doesn't show: feelings of unmatchable peace and liberation; hours of wandering around the hills in my father's footsteps; our big family gathering, with the men cutting up the meat and the feast at the banquet table set up out front; the smell and taste of roast pork; laughter, *tamburica* music, songs, and my mother's encouragement to do the banned "Ljepa Naša Domovina" ("My Beautiful Homeland"); the memory of my half-uncle Ivek in an ironed white shirt, mumbling like he always did, as though he had marbles in his mouth: "*Brzo, žedan sam ko graba*" ("quick, I'm thirsty like a ditch"); men sitting and women serving, and Štefek stubbornly refusing to leave his work for a family photo.

The author and his father roasting a pig in Srebrnjak, 1977.

The pig roast or its equivalent is at the heart of Croat life and will not soon die out. Friends and family will always get together for such big festive moments to mark the passage of time: the end of a seasonal cycle like the harvesting of wheat or grapes, a saint's day (or someone's name's day), a wedding, baptism, or holiday. These ceremonies celebrate life. The pig roast is the site for a collective wish for more life, an appreciation of the past, a dream of deferring death, the object of a shared labour, and a way to stay together as a family and enjoy an afternoon.

The cemetery in Molvice where my grandmother is buried rests on a table of land surrounded by hills. My father and I have come to the cemetery, not out of affection for the woman herself but out of curiosity about the dates on the headstone.

My father was just two when his mother crossed the hills from Srebrnjak to Molvice in 1945 to marry again. She left him, his brother, and his half-brother with her brother-in-law, uncle to the boys. Her first husband, my father's father, had died in 1942 while fighting for fledgling Croatia's regular army, the Domobrani (Home Guard), and like other war widows in impoverished Yugoslavia, she couldn't support her children. Her new husband was a widower with three kids of his own and didn't want any more, so she went to Molvice alone and never came back. When my father's uncle died less than a year later, his wife—Mila's mother, Slava—raised all the kids, including her three daughters. Yet somehow Slava managed, having the advantage of children grown old enough to work in the fields.

My grandmother's decision was unique in this area, though not unheard of around the country. People here still remember her somewhat infamous story. During my grandmother's wedding party at her brother-in-law's house, she sang and danced, appearing unperturbed by the gossip around her. The kids woke up from the noise and began crying. My father remembers following her to the top of Srebrnjak hill and being bribed with a few dinars to go back home. Only later, when she was an old widow and alcoholic pauper still living in the Husta house with her step-son, did my grandmother show any regret.

She needed my father then. I remember her frenetic drunkenness, the shrieking in the dingy bedroom. Even then, at her weakest, she was relentless. "My son, my son," she wailed, prefacing each descent into her miseries while he stood listening, paralyzed. She wanted him to take her to Canada but he refused.

On the way to the cemetery, we see the three-storey Husta house that her step-son passed onto his niece—a trollop, they say, who left her husband and two kids for a boyfriend who convinced her to sell all the land and spend it on vacations to Montenegro and the Black Sea. Neither she nor anyone else in the family spent the money to engrave the death dates on the grey granite headstones of the last three Hustas, including my grandmother. As a result, there's no finality to their lives, as if they'd gone missing or were still alive somewhere. I take some photos and we drive in the direction of Okić.

I've seen this arrow-headed hill with its ruined castle from the top of Srebrnjak. For the first time in my life, I'll drive towards it, exploring the area beyond the immediate vicinity of our home valley. There isn't anything remarkable about this trip, but it excites me anyway. So

Wooden house (ca. 1900), with newer, unfaçaded one behind, on way towards Okić (Prigorje), 1999.

much waits to be seen in the twisting turns of narrow roads leading us higher and higher. Eventually, we come to one of the last hamlets below Okić, Podgradje (which literally means "under the city").

Podgradje consists of a few houses and barns on a dead-end road. Right off the road there's a straw and manure heap behind a barn. The hindquarters of a beige cow are visible through a doorway and pigs are rooting in a rickety wooden enclosure. As I snap some pictures, a few villagers notice my car's German plates and stop to say hello. They're smiling and intrigued that a German would want to photograph one of their forgettable animals. When I explain my purpose in coming to Croatia, a man with a handlebar mustache and a cigarette hanging out the side of his mouth goes into the barn and leads out a chocolate-coloured horse. Although it's his old neighbour's, he doesn't feel out of place showing it himself. The villagers look proud there's still a horse around; it's the last one in the whole area and seems to belong to everybody.

The horse's owner is seventy-five-year-old Ivan Domović, a short, powerful man with a tanned, lined face and wisps of white hair on his head. He invites us to his cellar for a glass of wine. The cellar is a low

The cow in its barn in Podgradje (Prigorje), 1999.

wooden building, about a century old, down a grassy path across from the barn. In its moist space are huge barrels set against the walls. The light bulb is about as strong as a toy train's, revealing the dim outlines of saws and other tools hanging from the rafters. I ask Ivan about the black bicycle leaning against one of the barrels.

"Sure I drive it. Not as much, but I still drive it to Samobor." He used to transport sacks of wheat to the mill, loading it on his handlebars. "Going down was no sweat. Coming up was tough. Had to walk most of the way."

Life hasn't changed much for him and his wife. It's the last year of the century, but they're following the same patterns as they did in the middle of it. In fact, he thinks they were better off before. "Everybody had a job in Yugoslavia. We got credit. We bought machinery, supplies. Now the government just steals from us. Thieves, that's all."

Ivan's fourteen-year-old neighbour, Danijel Držanić, is listening in on the conversation. He's handsome and has a sure way about him but none of the machismo or swagger of other Croat boys his age. I ask him about life here and he surprises me. "We have everything we want. Good air, good food, good company. Why live in Zagreb?"

"Don't young people want to get out, leave this life?" I ask.

"Some of them do. But not me."

"Isn't it boring?"

"Why boring? There's always something happening, someone to talk to. We're friends here. He's like my grandfather."

"I'll ask you again in ten years."

"You can do that. I'll be here where I like it."

Ivan's wife, Štefica, arrives to say hello. She's pretty and slim, with curly grey hair and lively eyes like fireflies trapped in her head. I ask her about the *nošnje* peasants used to wear. "Some *bake* still wear them. Not the old men. There's not many alive anyway. Maybe you can find the old people higher up," and she waves her arm vaguely in the direction of the Okić. "But," she adds hopefully, "I can put on my *nošnje* so you can photograph me!"

The sun sets while we talk. Now, with the light failing, the bulb weakly carves these brown faces into the earthy shapes of van Gogh's potato-eaters, but without that impoverished, beaten-down quality, the desperate attachment of peasants to the earth. These people have electricity, running water, pensions, and get supplies in the local store. A few have satellite dishes. Many used to work, or still do, in factories in the mornings and on the land the rest of the day. They seem content and healthy here. They won't soon beg their way to another country or ignore the death dates on their families' headstones.

The peasant widow sits on an oak chopping block in front of her house. Summer days she spends watching the goings-on along the little road, chucking pieces of conversation at neighbours on their way to some job in their fields or vineyards. (Ivančići is one of seventeen hamlets in the hilly district of Sveta Jana, known for its wine production.) She's wearing a black kerchief, blouse, and skirt, all well past clean and spotted by dirt and food. Her hands lean on the cane she uses to get around. The few teeth in her mouth make her smile more of a cackle.

North of Jastrebarsko and bordering on the Žumberak, Sveta Jana is a collusion of twisting roads and deep valleys that are only physically hard to reach and withhold no secret from travellers once they get here. People are open and friendly. Most are peasants living a step more backwardly than those in Podgradje or Srebrnjak, as if the negligibly few extra miles from the metropolis and the obtruding hills have slowed modernity.

I see a woman carry a wooden *korito* to a pool, dump out her clothes, and beat them clean against the bowl, her right arm windmilling down from behind her head. Her head is swathed tightly in a red kerchief, knotted in a bow at the nape of her neck, and she wears a pleated skirt down to her ankles. A horse-drawn leiter-wagon goes by carrying a pig in a steel cage. The skinny peasant driving looks like a taut rope straining a heavy load; his big knotty hands are rooted in sinewy rawhide, and red capillaries have burst across his honed cheeks. Delicate on the reins, he flickers a toothy grin of gold bits on the way past.

Down from the widow's place are two large nineteenth-century stone houses—one bearing a Latin blessing on a stone tablet, the other formerly belonging to a lawyer who was the richest man in the village. Its stone is now crumbling and the basement is occupied by a destitute single mother of two. More typically throughout Sveta Jana are stubby wooden dwellings of the sort my father was born in, and that Štefek and Mila moved out of in the early 1970s—unadorned, sometimes plastered white, perched in rows on the spines of hills or crouching in valleys amid newer houses whose owners haven't quite quit farm life. The widow's own house is formerly well-to-do; its two storeys are built on stone, with a sagging wooden balcony entwined by creepers.

Barbara Skačan is all smiles, but she watches the camera closely. "I'm just an old woman, so why take a picture of me?" she shrugs, making sure not to smile for the photograph. Fifty years ago, in more superstitious times, she might have crossed herself. She tells me she lives on her own; her sons and two grandchildren live nearby and are in touch every once in a while. She raised the two youngsters from the cradle while their parents were working in Germany.

Inside, she offers me red wine from a twenty-litre glass demijohn. I notice an archaic wooden dish rack screwed into the wall by a steel sink and, incongruously, modern taps that run water in from the well. In a cloudy glass of water floats a clove of garlic, a concoction to lower her blood pressure. The living room is also the bedroom. Spacious enough by peasant standards, it speaks of a class hierarchy that has no bearing on nor correlation with the house or her life now. There are large framed photos of her sons in Yugoslav Air Force and Tito's Guard uniforms, various pictures of the Madonna and Jesus, rosaries in plastic cups, and crucifixes hanging around the frames, probably put there to protect her boys. A beautiful tan armoire of pear wood sags against one wall. She says it came with her as her dowry when she married into the family sixty years ago. The place is cozy, and it smells of mould, wine cellars, mothballs, and garlic.

As I examine the photos, she confides, "I had heartburn in both pregnancies, like poison ivy, so I knew the babies'd have lotsa hair. And there you see, see?" She points a black fingernail at the heads. The priest baptized the kids when they were two days old so they could go safely out into the world, and she took their clothes off the line before dusk so bad spirits wouldn't invade them.

A young man arrives in the kitchen. He wears a white polo shirt and sunglasses on his head. His face is leanly handsome and cocky, backing up into something else when he sees me. "What's *he* doing here?" he asks her. He is one of her grandsons. He looks at the air between his outstretched hands and, when I explain my presence there, says, "What are you doing *here*?" He retreats down the steps ahead of me, evidently leaving as well, his stiff smile adrift like a guest come to the wrong door. I learn he's a career military man like his father and uncle, but not entirely loyal to a government he admits provided him and others jobs by increasing military spending. "So far they knew they could count on our votes," he adds distastefully. He's done better for himself than one might imagine for a mere private, judging by the white Suzuki SUV parked in front of the house. As I drive off, I see him shaking hands with friends down the road and, in the rear-view mirror, I spot the widow back on the chopping block, watching.

■

Christmas Eve in 1996 is cold. Samobor huddles under a steel sky at the base of the Samobor hills, which ripple and enfold Srebrnjak. The city lies fifteen kilometres southwest of Zagreb through the flat Sava River valley, over the same ground as the original road built by

Napoleon during his rule between 1809 and 1813, when Samobor was the centre of a canton in his Illyrian provinces. The highway was rebuilt by the Nazis during World War Two, and stretches of their work are still intact. On the southern side of the road used to stand the trees from which Tito's Partisans hanged Ustaše, Domobrani, and other "dissidents" in the new regime. The Communist Party of Croatia was established in Samobor in 1937 and the Žumberak hills became its stronghold.

But Samobor bears no signs of this turbulence, so scarless and pretty is the face it presents to the world. Partly destroyed by a fire in 1797, it was rebuilt in the image of an Austrian town, with its ochre façades, steep slanted roofs, and secluded mansions in the woods.

From the bus station, I walk past a queue of locals waiting for meat or cheese pies and soft pretzels glazed with salt, through the market where vendors persistently greet me with "Izvolite" (at your service), and past butcher shops where huge smoked hams, smoked sausages, and clusters of pork hocks hang on hooks.

I've come to Samobor partly to catch a glimpse of the aging peasants from surrounding villages who usually arrive at dawn every Saturday. Most are stooped, kerchiefed women who get rides from their sons or grandsons now. Forty years ago, they used to trudge to Tresnjevačka market on the outskirts of Zagreb, twenty or more kilometres away, arriving on time by leaving in the middle of the night. Poverty made people walk great distances for a few dinars.

The three babas defying this wintry Christmas Eve don't appear as poor. They're selling bottles of liquor and curling stones of dried homemade cheese. So bundled in coarse wool coats, scarves wound around their heads, they're rendered almost immobile, like kids in snowsuits. Only their eyes are active: charcoal bits peering out from pale oval faces, their noses dimpled like old potatoes. In summer, it's easier to tell where old women such as these originate, like those from Slani Dol, who wear their characteristic white kerchiefs, aprons, and flowery dresses.

"What's this?" I ask, since none of the women has hounded me.

"That," one answers, "is *rakija*" (brandy). There's a moment of silence; then, remembering to sell me the bottle, she goes on. "That is *loza*, very good, very pure." I get the feeling that these women are out here more for social reasons than to make a buck. She unscrews the cap with her thick, cracked hands and fills it. "*Izvolite.*"

I sip it down. It's brandy all right, a wine flavour instead of plum. Feeling guilty for not buying her five-dollar bottle (since I have Štefek's supply), I slink away and meander through the rest of the market. On tables everywhere are plastic dishes sprouting delicate green wheat. Catholic tradition here is that on December 13, Sveta Lucia's name's day, wheat seeds are first watered to symbolize Christ's birth and new life in general. The fish shop offers Dalmatian cod or squid for those serving a meatless dinner during the day; many people are following custom again since the death of officially atheist Yugoslavia. Traditionally, a complete meal follows midnight Mass and usually involves a familiar pariah, a turkey.

Lean Christmas trees and stands selling cards and cheap baubles are stuffed in the narrow alley leading to Kralj Tomislav Square. *Tamburica* jingle bells are playing from a speaker. In the oak-beamed Samoborski Klet, you can hear traditional music, of the Christmas season and otherwise. A well-known local song is "Samoborci Piju Vino z Lonci" ("Samoborci Drink Wine from Pots"). A chorus of women begins cheerfully, "If I could choose boys, I wouldn't know which to choose." Then the men cut in, "Samoborci drink wine from pots, what they have they give for wine," and finally the women lament in conclusion, "I wouldn't choose one of them, wouldn't choose one of them, wouldn't choose one of them!"

"And we're sitting there drinking wine and eating prosciutto, and this chicken comes into the house. I couldn't believe it. Right into the house and then back out the door. I laughed. I never saw anything like that before." So says Hockey Hall of Famer Frank Mahovlić over the phone as he describes his visit to his parents' native hamlet of Gornji Mahovlići in 1972.

Mahovlić played for the Toronto Maple Leafs, Detroit Red Wings, and Montreal Canadiens from 1956 to 1974. Along with his brother, Peter, he participated in the Cold War hockey summit against the Soviet Union in September 1972.

"In Yugoslavia they were fifty years behind. I saw women still washing clothes in a dammed-up creek," Mahovlić tells me.

He and his wife drove into the Žumberak hills west of Samobor on the border with Slovenia. The house belonging to his mother's brother displayed three pictures on the wall: each of the Mahovlić sons in their hockey uniforms, and their sister in her wedding dress. When Frank and his wife returned later in the evening for dinner, other villagers and relatives showed up to greet him. "Peter's son has come back," they said. The women began to cry. His parents were dead, having long ago emigrated to Canada, where he himself was born, so he and his brother were the last contacts.

"And we had this big fried chicken dinner. It was the same chicken that walked into the house in the afternoon!" Frank never went back.

I decide to brave the relentless turns into the Žumberak. At first, the forest of oak, walnut, beech, and maple trees nearly swallows the car, but once I am out of the forest's maw, the country opens up onto a plateau where the land is cultivated and hamlets appear. The owner of a grocery store by a tiny fork in the road, where a couple of young farmers just off their tractor are drinking beer, figures out where I want to go and draws me a map. I chat for a while with the men. None of them has heard of Frank Mahovlić.

Sheep in the grassy enclosure across the road are grazing in the shade. Further on is a trout hatchery, and beside the road is an eight-foot-high gravestone choked by trees, the tablet reading, *Nikolaus Ritter von Weymann, 1858*. No one at the hatchery knows about this Austrian knight either. Eventually, after an hour of slow driving from Samobor, I reach another plateau, where a village is set against the late-afternoon sun. A brand-new sign in flowing script reads, *Welcome to Gornji Mahovlići*.

The hamlet is a surprise: very old, quiet, and tidy. There are new houses, of course, but many older brick or wooden peasant dwellings, manicured lawns, vegetable gardens, and flowers by the thousands, as if locals were readying for a wedding—or a funeral.

The woman with mahogany-dyed hair whom I ask for information thinks a minute before walking decisively but unsteadily down the gravel street in her cork-heeled *natikače* sandals. She leads me to a patchwork

*Ladder and barn in Gornji Mahovlići (Prigorje),
1999.*

peasant house of brick and concrete blocks embedded with wood
windows and a door scratched with graffiti. Mahovlić's mother was
born here. A young farmer next door has the key, and we enter a
kitchen streaming with sunlight, floored by sagging grey wood.

"... and this chicken comes into the house." The scene flickers to
life: laughter and memories and tears, then the bird stepping nervously
on stage. The picture goes dark. There's no sign of the photos.

My guide points down the street to a stone peasant house: Mahovlić's
father's. Such houses are uncommon in northern Croatia and virtually
all are found in Lika, in Istria, or on the coast. The house looks like it
will stand another century. In contrast, just before it is the only rundown

place in the village; chickens and turkeys live in the basement's former wine cellar. A woman wearing near-rags comes out, then hurries inside when she sees me approaching. Grapevines choke the front and chamomile hangs from the roof to dry. Out front stands a crucifix encased by glass under a narrow tin roof, once the sign of the village centre, back when the house had a prominent position.

Although many left Gornji Mahovlići and never came back, and the generation born outside Croatia has little sentimentalism for it, those born here are still loyal. A new house with a North American double garage, built by Mahovlić's distant cousin, sits at the top of the hamlet. The family stays for months on end in these secluded Žumberak hills. Their friends call them crazy for not building a place on the coast. But their reasons could be simple: good air, good food, and good company. My own attachment to Prigorje is founded on such things, even though I wasn't born there. The distance I've travelled emotionally from my father's home isn't as great as it is for other descendants of immigrants. If Croatia is a borderland country, between east and west, then perhaps I too can be defined in similar terms, with one foot in Canada and one here. Now, unfamiliar regions of the country, like Zagorje, are tugging at me.

4 ■ ZAGORJE
Of Heartlands and Hagiography

THE DENSELY POPULATED REGION OF ZAGORJE, north of Zagreb and on the other side of Medvednica Mountain, has been mythologized by some Croats as the heartland of Croatia, like the Midwest in the United States. But Zagorje (which literally means "behind the hills") got this status neither by default, since other regions could make the same claim, nor because it's unique. Zagorje doesn't look unique, resembling Prigorje and most of northern Croatia with its mix of flat farmland and hills, orchards, vineyards, villages nestled in valleys, and houses fronted by iron gates. Maybe this generic quality has made the region seem quintessentially Croat. For me Zagorje is worth visiting because of its remaining peasant settlements and because of the significant political and cultural leaders it has produced.

Although the Zagorci speak a particular dialect of Croatian called *kajkavski*, which distinguishes them, it's safe to say they aren't radically different from people elsewhere in the country. Nevertheless, their apparent differences have been concentrated by others, paradoxically, into a stereotype that probably originated in the rural past.[1] The typical Zagorac is the country hick who goes blind once a day from too much bad wine. He's hard-working, friendly, easily led, not very brave, and violent when crossed; he has disputes over land caused by Zagorje's overcrowding and makes the worst husband (in contrast, women from Zagorje are said to make the best wives). I've met peasants and workers from other areas who fit the description. The fact the stereotype hasn't quite died leads one to believe either that life in Zagorje hasn't changed all that much or that peasant life as it was endures on a quasi-mythical or ideological level throughout the country.

In crowded Zagorje, the *zadruga* offers further insight into the origins of the stereotype and into the peasant's character as it might still exist.[2] In this old clan structure or patriarchal collective, peasants tilled the land in common under the rule of the *Gospodar* (head man). According to Tito, who grew up in a *zadruga*, the patriarch "lived in the biggest house, in which everybody ate together. When a member of the zadruga married, the zadruga would build him a special little room attached to the big house, so that the whole zadruga looked like a beehive."[3] The *zadruga* instilled the value of close family bonds, believed to ward off poverty (especially of single-family living); it also instilled the values of non-monetary wealth, respect towards elders, the importance of duty, and acceptance of one's rank. Every individual was restrained by the "superintendence of those about him"; he had a "dignity to preserve," a "position and a name," and the "proverb 'noblesse oblige' is not without its application to him."[4]

But the *zadruga* was sometimes a brutal patriarchy in which women had little recourse against violent husbands, and girls tended to be treated poorly compared to boys. The superintendence of others and "noblesse oblige" were likely means of limiting counter-intuitive thinking and mocking artistry. Superstition was entrenched, though often benign. For instance, some young women feared eating plums and peaches because they knew—or so they were told—they would then have twins. The best aspects of *zadruga* life may not be fully explicable to outsiders. For most peasants born into a collective, another life was probably inconceivable, and the repetitions of their lives were deeply, unconsciously comforting—to strike out on foot and horse-drawn wagon for a summer field and mow wheat together with sickles as they'd done since childhood, to sweat and cut hands, to drink wine and sing songs, and later to feast at the *Gospodar*'s home.

While the *zadruga* began to dissolve for good around the end of the nineteenth century, remnants of their social relations are still evident in rural Croatia. Family and neighbours count on each other for help, although sometimes they might pay for labour, gas, or the use of a tractor.

I got a feeling for this old way of life whenever I visited Croatia. I remember especially the hot, sleepy afternoons when we left for the hills, the jolting rides in wooden wagons and the wagons stacked so high on the return home with wheat or hay that we had to duck under tree branches; I remember the camaraderie, the relaxed steady labour, the breaks for *gemišt* (wine and mineral water), flies around my sweaty back, ticks on my ankle under my work socks, blisters and cuts on my hands, our satisfaction when the work was done (and my private happiness knowing I didn't have to work like this the rest of my life!). The old guy who drove us in his twenty-five-year-old John Deere was a big man with strong arms and white cropped hair who once said his neighbour's father was strong as a horse, but that his neighbour was only as strong as a mare (branding him *kobila* for the rest of his life). Slavko Jacopač got paid with food, wine and sometimes increasingly worthless Yugoslav dinars. When he got his money he lifted a bill mockingly to the sun to see it was real, then spat on the ground. Communism was shit, he told us. He told us other things too. He joked about his neighbours, gave me advice about life, made vulgar comments to the women working with us. They smiled wanly, neither wanting to encourage him by laughing nor wanting to appear insulted, because that would mean they couldn't take his jokes or didn't grasp the spirit in which he talked (which was supposed to be friendly). They were used to him by now because he'd helped them for years. For me, he added to the relaxed atmosphere of jokes, banter, gossip, politics, philosophy, and history that made the work go quickly, kept people on their toes and even, ultimately, brought them closer together.

One debatable stereotypical trait of the Zagorac is that he's easily led. After all, two of Croatia's and Yugoslavia's "strong men" came from Zagorje. My father likes to joke that only two Zagorci ever went to school, but that both became president. The two were Tito and Franjo Tudjman (1923–1999).

Tito was born in 1893 in the village of Kumrovec near the Slovenian border, to a Slovene mother and Croat father. His birthday was celebrated on May 25 (the same day, incidentally, as my mother's, who was born in a German bunker during Allied bombing in World War Two). Numerous accounts of his life paint a picture of restless youth and travels in search of work, often resulting in socialist agitation, as well as contempt for authority (except his own, of course). His name is a matter of speculation. The Ustaše apparently claimed that TITO stood for Tajna Internacionalna Teroristička Organizacija (Secret International Terrorist Organization); Churchill's special envoy to Yugoslavia during the war, Fitzroy MacLean, said the name derived from the way he ordered subordinates: "You do this. You, this" (*Ti, to*). In *Tito Speaks*, Tito himself said he took the name from the eighteenth-century Croat writer Tito Brezovački, and that the name was a common one in the Kumrovec region. As Brian Hall wrote, it "seemed superbly indicative of Yugoslavia that something as easily verifiable as this last explanation had never been verified."[5]

I went to verify it. There was no evidence in church records of Tito's claim. None of the old people I spoke to ever knew or heard of another Tito besides Josip Broz. No biographies substantiate the rumour that he'd gotten the name during the Spanish Civil War, but some suggest he emerged instead from Serbia's Karadjordjević-run Yugoslav prisons in Maribor and Lepoglava (1929–1934) as Tito in order to conceal his identity. Such conflicting speculations may once have veiled the identity of the man, part of a fortuitous and probably deliberate mystification or legend-making that went on even after his death.

I remember walking into stores in the late 1980s in search of his image—invariably on the walls, sometimes in the form of photos, other times in bas-reliefs or sketches. I had this idea of setting up a museum consisting only of Tito pictures. Mischievously, I would ask salespeople why his picture was on the wall, and whether I could have it. Usually they claimed they hadn't noticed it and always answered no, eyeing me carefully as if I were either dangerous or a fool. Even ten years after his death, people were still reticent about removing his image, although it was no longer Tito they feared.

In 1990, images of Tito disappeared. But Marino Tartaglio's 1947 portrait of the leader in his olive-green marshal's uniform continued to hang in Croatia's Gallery of Modern Art, a sombre picture of the already stout leader with scar-like marks on his face, which seemed to signify the battles he'd been through. People wept in Croatia and across Yugoslavia when he died. He was the only leader many knew, a father figure they'd been taught to love, a man still respected by many even now. A proverb of sorts had grown up around him: "After Tito—Tito."

The second leader to come out of Zagorje, Franjo Tudjman, was born in Veliko Trgovišće, near Kumrovec. The proximity of his birth-place to Tito's seems appropriate since his career was closely bound to Tito's. He was once Tito's general. And his prisoner. He was locked up for two years after his involvement with Matica Hrvatska's program of Croat linguistic revival and the nationalist insurgency, called the Croatian Spring of 1971, and then again from 1981 to 1983 for inter-views given most famously in the diaspora newspaper *Hrvatska Država* (Croatian State), wherein he questioned the statistical high number of Serb dead in Ustaša concentration camps during World War Two. He said this number had ultimately served Serbian political interests at the expense of Croatia's. When the moment was ripe in 1989, he founded the political party Hrvatska Demokratska Zajednica (Croatian Democratic Union) and eventually won the presidency in Croatia's first post-communist elections. He had suffered for his views and his nationalist pedigree was ripe for the times.

Had Tito and Tudjman died earlier, their historical importance to their own people would have been very different and perhaps more secure. Tito was condemned by all sides for being a dictator who held the country together through gulags like Goli Otok (naked island), for crushing nationalism and fragmenting territorial integrity (he was never forgiven by Croats for the massacre of Domobran and Ustaša soldiers at Bleiburg after World War Two), and for siphoning off the wealth of the country's more productive regions in order to support the poorer ones and finance a Serb-dominated infrastructure (while he and his cronies lived the good life). Yet he has been credited with loosening his hold on the country, writing into the 1974 constitution, for instance, each republic's right to self-determination, which laid the groundwork for Croatia's separation from Yugoslavia in 1991.

Tudjman fell by becoming the don of a mafia-type organization that sold state-owned companies at bargain-basement prices to interests supposedly unrelated to the government, which oversaw a significant decline in living standards among the working and lower classes. While Tudjman can't be blamed for everything that went wrong in the transition from communism to capitalism, he can be criticized for his government's corruption and Croatia's increased isolation from the west. He can't be blamed for getting old, but he can be held accountable for his stale political philosophy—which was stuck around 1943, determined by the threat of the Serb "Other."

Tito failed because he murdered too much and couldn't live forever. Tudjman failed because he tried to be Tito and had neither the charisma nor the vision. You can only wrap yourself in the *šahovnica* and fear-monger for so long. Once Serbia ceased to be a threat, his own identity became compromised.

The degree to which Tudjman aspired to, yet tried to outdo the hagiography of Titoism became apparent when the restored house where he was born was opened to the public in 1998. A Zagreb daily called the *Jutarnji List* devoted a page to a mocking comparison of Tito's house and Tudjman's. Tito's, the article noted, is closer to the nineteenth-century original, with a cast iron stove and some basic peasant furniture. In contrast, Tudjman's has been redone to look like a Hapsburgian upper-class house, complete with baby-blue façade, chandelier, and washroom. The joke is that his father's ghost came back and said, "Francek, my son, what's going on here? There are gold faucets in the bathroom. I thought we never even had a bathroom, boy!"

As I drive between Kumrovec and Veliko Trgovišće, the sky is spotless and the sun, like a scalpel, defines every contour of the hills. Roads meander pleasantly from village to village. In Vilanci, I notice a diminutive wooden house washed baby blue. It has wooden shutters and flowerpots between the windows, blooming geraniums and daisies. Each end of the house is made of vertical brown planks punctured by a single hole in the shape of a heart—decorations and air vents for the attic, where corn and such was stored. This house is Franjo Tudjman's—minus the gold faucets.

The peasant woman in her yard (Zagorje), 1999.

A woman steps outside when she notices me taking a picture. She has a jowly basset-hound face brightened by eczema, and she wears a Mother Hubbard, a blue kerchief, and brown imitation-felt slippers with rubber soles. "There's not much to see," she says cheerfully, showing me around. "My husband died and now I'm alone." Yet next door live her daughter and son-in-law, who help her get by. If I go door to door, I'll probably find one elaborate clan that will grow tenuous at the village's outskirts, only to be replaced by another.

Her yard is a confusion of chicken coops, pigsties, stacked wood, greying vineyard poles, hoes, pitchforks, a water pump, a well, and two discarded wood stoves. A whetstone in its sheath is a sign of her husband. So too is an authentic German World War One helmet with a *šahovnica* on the front, decorated by some kids but possibly a sign of the old man's political sympathies during those years. The impression I get from her place is that it's evidence of the hamlet as it looked decades ago, before it grew into a village and new houses replaced the old. You have to leave the flatlands for the hills to get a feel for the past (as it exists now).

To that end, I drive up a rutted road hardly wider than the car, toward a church high on a hill. Oak, walnut, and beech trees shade the way, and views open up onto valleys full of vineyards. I imagine peasants winding along this path behind a bride and groom; I can hear the strumming of tamburicas and voices breaking into song. Someone dressed as Green George leads villagers on his name's day, April 23, draped in branches and blessing houses with a twig as priests do at Christmas.

The church I noticed from the valley is bounded by a graveyard of simple wooden or rusted iron crosses, and grandiose granite sarcophagi and headstones. Families have spent enormous amounts of money here—in some cases, their life savings. Klanječko Jezero is a tiny pocket of a valley a few hundred yards downhill from the cemetery; its villagers won't likely end up in expensive granite vaults. Two dirty, white wooden houses lie below. I walk down the grass path and enter the wooden gate of the first.

The woman who opens the door a fraction looks at me carefully through cold, steady eyes. Josipa Šipek, born in 1923 *ispod brega* (under the hill), isn't so much afraid as cautious. She relaxes after I explain my reasons for coming to Croatia, and tells me that her husband bought this house "over there" and moved it one hundred yards to this spot. "I'm all alone here," she says. "My husband died last year." But like the woman I met earlier, she's not entirely alone because her three daughters live in nearby villages and attend to her regularly.

Under a lean-to is another collection of tools, along with four old wagon wheels off the horse-drawn hay cart that her husband used to negotiate down the steep path to the barn. Closer to the house is a narrow brick structure like an outhouse, which turns out to be a kitchen where slop is made and stored for her pigs. The grass is cropped and a large apple tree spreads its shade across the yard. Nailed to the small, sagging barn are two birdhouses built by her husband. Looking around, I confirm once more my feeling that while no peasants I know ever formulated their artistry consciously or in conventional artistic terms, many seemed to have let humble objects like birdhouses or the natural settings in which they lived act as replacements for art.

She lets me in her house. There are three small rooms arranged in a row, like in a trailer home. The plastered ceiling is low, floorboards sinking in places, the original iron oven cemented into a wall. There are the usual framed pictures of the Madonna and Jesus. She has no running water, instead filling up a steel pail in the spring out back and washing clothes—and perhaps herself—in the tub outside. She has an outhouse, electricity, and a twenty-three-inch colour TV, which lets her while away boring days watching American and Mexican soaps like most peasant women in Croatia, some who are illiterate, can't read the subtitles, but follow the plot by watching the gestures. I'm reminded of an old woman in Prigorje who's never grasped the phenomenon of acting. For her, the line between performance and reality is blurred, and television characters are actually real people. As if to confirm this confusion, she was woken one night by the thudding bass of a passing car's radio and thought it was the TV. Annoyed, she drawled, "*Vrag ti taj televizor jebal, ter ti ga jebal*" ("may the devil fuck you, TV, may he fuck you").

Having finished her lunch and her beer, Josipa offers me cheese strudel just out of the oven. It is all she has to give me. Her generosity, however, doesn't extend to the wiry little man I saw pacing in front of the house behind hers. She looks at me strangely when I mention wanting to speak to him, and her face regains some of its coldness.

Her neighbour slips inside and closes the door when I approach his place. There's a sad little garden in front and a stream bubbling into the woods. He finally sticks his head out the door, so I coax him into the yard and we start a conversation. He wears a grey work shirt and jeans rolled up at the bottom. Up close his face looks delicate and pointed, his grey hair in need of a trim. He's younger than Josipa, born in 1945, but lives in worse conditions.

"This is just a shack. You should talk to somebody else," he complains in a high voice. "You can see for yourself, I got nothing." He flings his arms outwards. "In the winter, my pension lets me eat once a day. How can you live like that?"

His brief stint at a nearby textile factory, which collapsed in 1991, didn't let him accrue a more sizeable pension. Now he's fifty-four, relying on government handouts and not looking for work, apparently. These financial troubles make him nostalgic for the Yugo days. "Tito's death was a bad thing. Croatia got nothing from him. But it was a bad thing," he argues confusedly. "Aahhhhh," he exclaims, *"nisam pop niti comunista!"* (I'm neither a priest nor a communist).

I want to view the inside of his house to see what he's ashamed to show. The rooms are arranged like Josipa's but smaller. The one on the left has a TV, a cot piled halfway to the ceiling with dirty laundry, and a portrait of a young woman in the photo-sketch technique that used to be popular.

"What's your name?" I ask.

"Mira Burek. I was nineteen then," she says, pointing at the portrait.

What a surprise! I've been talking to a woman! Her posture, work shirt, and jeans fooled me, since I've never seen a peasant woman wear them. I get the feeling that her eccentricity has left her an outsider here, if her neighbour's coldness is any indication.

In the middle room, the kitchen, is a plastic demijohn for water, a portable steel basin, and a small fridge plastered with yellowing stickers of Yugo comic characters, Dinamo Zagreb, and Red Star Belgrade soccer stars long since retired. The son who pasted these when he was a kid now lives in a large Austrian-style house fifty yards away. Mira was divorced years ago and evidently is on poor terms with her boy. I don't ask about her husband.

The last room is a storage area housing a wooden cage filled with young turkeys. The stink is terrible. The house as a whole feels like a grungy basement apartment somewhere in Zagreb, in contrast to Josipa's healthier, albeit primitive, peasant's place.

"My land goes down to the house there. The water's mine too, mine all mine."

"But the woman below uses the water, doesn't she?"

"Aaahhh, what can I do? Her axe fell into the honey. We don't talk," she adds, wagging a finger. They were having a dispute over land, so perhaps the stereotype of the Zagorac has some bearing on reality after all. Then again, I think, put people close together long enough anywhere in the world and there will be conflict.

As I leave, she comes closer and whispers, "Don't tell anyone you were here. No one should know you were here. No one, hear?"

"They won't," I promise.

■

Zagorje's main town, Krapina, lies at the bottom of a confluence of forested hills and has a familiar Austrian character. But Krapina's identity is bound to its Croat origins. Since 1966, it has been the site every September of a festival celebrating northern Croatia's *kajkavski* culture and language, as tamburica ensembles play and dance to folk songs like "Meknite Se, Vse Gore":

> Move away all the mountains
> So Zagorje can be seen
> So you can see the cradle
> That I was rocked in.

On the cloudy day when I arrive, workers are refaçading the church by the highway and sheathing its steeple's crown and gables' roofs with new copper. The most recent past, with all its architectural deadification and memories, is constantly being elided in favour of a more distant past—the beginnings, the cradle of Croat identity. It seems correct that Krapina's most famous citizen, the Illyrian Ljudevit Gaj, fostered Croatia's mid-nineteenth-century nationalism, although it was tempered by stronger ties with Serbia.[6]

In leaving Zagorje, it strikes me that the hamlets and villages dotting the place, even the ones at the point of complete dissolution where only a few old women remain, played and may still play a role in the rise of its significant leaders. Here was an agrarian populace that inspired loyalty in its politicians, yet arrogance as well. I suspect that the density of the region made it a more monolithic voting body that could be manipulated.

A cousin of mine who works in Krapina's cardiac surgery clinic once told me this: "In villages, people are not so educated, and they are poisoned by ideas. Television has very big influence in such places. The politicians knew this and used it, not just here but in Serbia. None of this war was by accident, even though Serbian politicians tried to make it seem like a people's 'happening.'" This was not true, he said, his voice sounding incredulous. "People with no morals and nationalist ideas made people angry and afraid. If Goebbels had this possibility of TV propaganda, well then..." He trailed off, shaking his head. Turning his thoughts to Tudjman's regime, he added, "In politics, obviously you can play the national game till people have work and enough to eat. But when you have robbed them to poverty, it doesn't work anymore. Enough of national talk behind which mafia makes dirty business."

How inevitable that the elderly and uneducated played a role of which they weren't fully aware until later. If there is an area of the country that has benefitted least from such manipulations by the first post-Yugoslav government, yet suffered most in the fight for independence, it could be Slavonia. What are people's attitudes now towards the nation and the blood price of its birth? I would soon find out.

5 ◧ SLAVONIA, POSAVINA
Return of the Storks

ON A THIRTY-FIVE-DEGREE DAY IN JULY 1999, MY
father and I point our rented car to the east and rip across the Slavonian
flatlands. Expanses of wheat- and cornfields stretch away on either
side of the highway as black oil hammerheads nod slowly. Distant
villages waver in the heat and hills periodically crumple the land.
Having grown up in Alberta, I intuitively understand the attraction in
the dull spaciousness of the region. Because Slavonia is mostly flat, it's
a good territory to invade and a tough one to defend.

At first, there are no signs of its violent past. The exit for Slavonska
Požega takes us through rolling countryside, interspersed by flatter
stretches with villages strung along the road unlike any I've seen so far
in Zagorje and Prigorje. Gone are two- or three-storey houses enclosed
by painted iron fences. These houses are set ten yards off the road,
small and squat, a couple of yards separating them. In some cases,
they are joined in rows as if huddling against winter's cold or colluding
against an enemy. The oldest houses aren't built of wood but rather
of a mouldering yellow brick. Yards are bare, unique for their wooden
stools under trees, where people sit, watch cars go by, or chat.

It may be that these villages reflect the nature of their inhabitants' social life, a close-knit communality left over from the *zadruga* that survived in Slavonia well into the twentieth century. I get the feeling that Slavonia's topography—its wide spaces—wasn't homologous with its social relations, that abundance of land pushed people closer together instead of apart.

Such closeness isn't always good. The war was here. Roofless brick carcasses periodically show up, sometimes two or three in succession among inhabited houses, which makes them seem more dead. "The Serbs aren't coming back," my father says. "You know those were the bastards."

"How do you mean?"

"They fought in the war, so people here know what they did."

"What they did?"

"They shot one of their neighbours or something and now they're afraid to come back."

At crossroads along the way stand tall concrete crucifixes, vaguely communist in their cold, functional style, quite unlike the soulful wooden crucifixes that now belong to another time. The newer ones seem unable to offer solace in face of this destruction.

We arrive in Slavonska Požega. This small, beautiful city has the spirit of Zagreb in parts; the spacious Jelačić-like main square is enclosed by similar baroque Austrian buildings built after Turkish rule (1536–1691). As if narrating a devolution from city to village, streets grow narrow off the square and buildings crouch together. Slavonska Požega seems always to have been a Croat town. On one building is inscribed *HR VAT * SKI DOM* 1897 (Croat Club), and numerous plaques honour Croat personalities. Western Slavonia's generally homogeneous ethnicity assures this identity, but further east near the Yugoslav border and south by the Sava River, on the border with Bosnia, Croat hegemony has been more in question.

Here, people are enjoying cool drinks at cafés, and life goes on innocuously. But it doesn't surprise me to overhear two men sitting by the main square talking seriously about politics. They're about to leave when we come, but they agree to stay when I ask them about the office of the Croatian Society for Political Prisoners around the block. "This is the guy you should talk to," the stout one tells me,

A street in Slavonska Požega (Slavonia), 1999.

pointing at his friend. The other is thin, with a lean, tanned face and wispy, sandy hair plastered on his head. He's wearing a white short-sleeved polyester shirt with an undershirt visible underneath, the uniform of older civil servants and intelligentsia.

"The office you're referring to holds the archives for Croats imprisoned in Yugoslavia, most notably around the Croatian Spring in 1971. Have you heard of the Croatian Spring?" the thin one asks me.

"I have."

"You're in luck," his friend tells me. "The man knows all about it. He was part of it."

"I am a professional politician," the thin guy laughs. "I worked side by side with the main personalities in this event, like Savka Dabčević-Kučar and Miko Tripalo, particularly in this region. I was arrested for organizing demonstrations, but they didn't have enough on me and let me go."

Dabčević-Kučar and Tripalo were prominent political figures within the Croatian Communist Party at the head of the upheaval, organizing student protests, negotiating with Tito for a loosening of ties with Yugoslavia, and addressing issues like the over-representation of Serbs in the military, police force, and important political positions. Under threats from Tito, who finally cracked down on the movement, they were expelled from the Communist Party but didn't serve prison sentences.

He hands me a laminated card, with Croatian on one side and English on the other: *Polytechnic of Požega. dr.sc. Antun Lovrić. Secretary.* "I'm still a professional politician," he says.

"But a socialist," interjects his friend.

"Well, he's HDZ. The far right."

"A Croat people's movement. The movement made the HDZ."

"But you're still friends," I interject.

"Sure, why not?" says Lovrić's friend, an electrical mechanic who worked for years in Germany but has difficulty speaking the language. "We're all Croats here." This comment gets at the heart of politics in the first years of independence. To win votes, parties outdid each other to assert their "Croatness." A decade later, they began to find other issues like the economy, or the morality of their leadership.

"If Ante Pavelić came back to life and walked past us, what would you do?" I ask them.

"Nothing. I'd shake his hand," the mechanic claims, with machismo.

"I dislike brutality," says Lovrić, disgusted. "This is a democratic Croatia. Tell the truth. No one is telling the truth. We need objective people to come to help determine the numbers."

I want to get a better sense of what they mean by Croat, how they define themselves. "We are a western people and we belong to Europe, where our mentality has always been oriented. As you may know, we were part of the Austro-Hungarian Empire. There are many differences between Croats and Serbs," Lovrić begins, listing them off. "Moral differences: kids still get married in Serbia because there's a patriarchal system in the Balkans. Physical differences: they have darker hair. Linguistic differences: we say *mlijeko* (milk) and they say *mleko*. It's clear, you can hear the difference: *mlijeko, mleko. Mlijeko, mleko.* The languages are completely different! Also, the Serbs are a military people, warrior-like...." He trails off. "There are so many differences, I would need days."

"And they're stupid," the mechanic whispers loudly, in pretend confidentiality.

Later at lunch my father says, "The stuff about language is weak. Sure there are some differences, like he was saying, but not that many. Don't you remember Štefek's comment? He understood Serbs in the army better than Zagorci, even though Zagorje is only twenty-five kilometres from Srebrnjak."[1]

The assurance Lovrić and his friend have about their Croat identity is striking to me because it's something I lack. Unlike them, my sense of national self has shifted depending on my location; here, I proudly call myself Canadian (and iconized this feeling by painting a maple leaf on that water trough in Srebrnjak). In Canada, I complain about always having to watch what I say (really being a Croat in temperament) and not being able to buy cheap beer and real smoked sausages. Yet some would call this hand-wringing about identity typically Canadian.

As I speak to these men in Slavonska Požega, I remember an incident that highlighted my unease with the absoluteness of their convictions. I was in the Croatian Hall in Vancouver with an immigrant from Herzegovina. As we crossed the foyer, music began and he tugged at my arm and ordered me to stop. No one could just carry on with the national hymn ("Ljepa Naša Domovina") playing. He and two other men put their hands on their hearts and turned to a large framed photo of Ante Pavelić, which hung on the wall. It was 1993 and Croatia had lost a third of its territory to the Serbs, so I sympathized a little with the desire to "kill the bastards." But I resented being obliged to participate in this ceremony by someone who'd snidely called me only one-quarter Croat because I was born in Canada and my mother was German. Ironically, he never volunteered to fight for Croatia, conveniently skirting that danger by saying his life was in Canada now and everyone back home was OK with that.

The drive leading from the former Highway of Brotherhood and Unity to Jasenovac in Posavina opens onto a small plain where an imposing commemorative monument in the form of stylized petals rises from the earth. The plain is empty of crops, but the sun is shining and swallows are flitting on the breezes.

Jasenovac is a sprawling village with no centre and no action. It reminds me of those grids of alleys in Canadian towns whose predictable layouts also indicate predictable lives. In the heat, it has fallen asleep, but dark shadows from the past disturb that slumber. It's the site of the infamous World War Two death camp run by the Ustaše. That was long ago, yet even in the 1990s Jasenovac was deemed important enough to have its own battle, even though nothing seemed worth fighting for. P.J. O'Rourke once wrote that after all the killing in Bosnia, the grand prize for the victors wouldn't be France or Italy, but Bosnia.

We drive around. I'd read that Jasenovac, as well as spots along the Bosna and Plitva rivers, the Slavonski Brod area, and Stara Gradiška, is still home to an ancient type of wooden house called *sojenice*. They were built on piles in wetland or in lake or riverbeds and date from the Iron Age. We see none of them. Some of the modern houses are plastered white, while others are covered by ordinary grey concrete, but most are naked brick. Bullet holes have strafed the walls and in the midst of inhabited homes are dead, roofless ones with trees growing out of their ground-floor windows. The Catholic church was hit hard but the steeple is caged in scaffolding and will soon be repaired.

At that point, I stop the car. Two storks are sitting on a chimney of a detonated house. They've come back home, as others have across Croatia now that it's peaceful again. Storks have always been considered good luck, so it's a hopeful sign to see them wisely perusing the town from their nest. Ironically, they've chosen this destroyed Serb place. They seem like the spirits of those people returned in this shape from exile, or death.

There are also signs of human life on Jasenovac's long main drag— a derelict red tractor, a white Fiat, a few mopeds, and some young guys drinking at a hole-in-the-wall café watching us sombrely. No one seems eager to talk as I get out to take a photograph; a cow in Podgradje breaks ice better than a Serb house in Jasenovac.

Further down, a family adding a section to their house is ready to knock off for the day. They're friendly and happy to chat, offering us wine and coffee. "Look around," says their neighbour, Marko Brnić, a slim blond man with a hard, cynical face. "We're all poor here. We don't have a hell of a lot. But what the fuck can we do, just go on living."

"We needed government money to help us rebuild this place. Half of it was gone after the war," adds the son of the family, Kruno Mareš.

"Sure the Serbs still live here!" laughs Brnić. "They've been here just as long as us. And they're better off. That's a Serb house, and that one there, see, façaded. Not like this one, or most of ours."

The grandmother heard us talking and came down the steps. She's barefoot, wears a black Mother Hubbard, and has an alert face. "Look at the boy's shirt," she says, gesturing at her grandson. "Gypsy rags."

"I guess things were better before," I say.

"Better before," she answers. "We had everything we needed. We worked hard. Before the big war, I remember we worked together. Families stayed together longer. I was young then, but I remember. People just lived."

"What about the camp? Did you know what was happening?"

"We never heard a sound."

"So you didn't see anything?" I ask.

"Nothing, nothing."

"But it's not a big village."

"They told us nothing." She looks straight into my eyes.

I ask them about the town's two churches. "You can see for yourselves. The one right there is the Serb one," says Brnić. It's a large white structure with two steeples topped by black cupolas. I see some marks like bullet holes, but decide not to check. "Our forces didn't touch their church. Now go visit ours."

The grandmother tells her grandson to take off his shirt. Long, raised scars like the sort left after shark bites, as well as round, pellet-size holes, decorate his chest. "Cluster bombs," he tells me matter-of-factly.

I look around the yard, at the brick barn and sties where the pigs are restlessly awaiting dinner. The grandmother tells me they will slaughter one soon because they're running out of meat. If they do it like in Srebrnjak, I know what it means, having held a leg once. The butcher, I remember, sharpened knives of varying lengths on a pedal-operated whetstone, taking a long time with the long knife. Then we coaxed the victim out of its sty. After it stood suspiciously and hesitantly in the light, it grunted into a clearing where someone had strewn fresh grass. There were four of us and we were on it immediately while the butcher roped the snout. Each of us clutched a shaking, kicking leg and kneeled against its epileptic sides while it squealed out its terror, the sound like a saw grinding through rusty metal. Then, when the knife stuck home, the squeal rose to a crescendo. We deposited the pig in a steel tub of boiling water, the water growing dirty pink as we scraped off hairs and knuckles. Then we hung it upside down on steel hooks and unzipped its stomach so the insides spilled out in bunches and coils of pink, purple, and red.

Because the sun is setting and we still have a few things to see, we say goodbye and drive half a mile south, as far as the road takes us. The road is guillotined at the Sava River. The bridge is a long slab of crumbling concrete lying across the water twenty yards below us. The far side is Bosnia. That's where the Serbs are. We can see and hear them swimming in the river, jumping off the banks—so close, but a world away. We're at a turn in a river that seems at the ends of the earth, a frontier where there's no crossing. Destroyed bridges in the former Yugoslavia are heavily symbolic. Many of them aren't being rebuilt, and that says something too.

We want to test the situation in Jasenovac, so we visit the Serbs Brnić pointed out to us. Down the lane from the Orthodox church, the house is one of the façaded ones. The grass in the yard is cropped and flowers are blooming in pots on the veranda. The old man sitting in the shade wears a crisp white shirt and wool pants; his hair is a snowy mane and his face very brown with high cheekbones. "*Dobar dan* (good day)," I call out to him.

"*Dobar dan.*" He gets up from his chair and walks over.

"I have some questions for you," I begin, stumbling into an inquisitory mode.

"Oh yes?" he replies, sounding unsure. I have this pressing need to put him at ease, which I didn't have with the Croats.

I explain my purpose in coming but before we can talk, his daughter emerges from the house. She carries herself with the same sort of formality as her father. She's around forty-five and has black, shoulder-length hair and a delicate aquiline nose. "What can I do for you?" she asks. She's suspicious and on the defensive. I ask some innocuous questions by way of a beginning.

"I get a pension from the government," the old man says. "I was an engineer. Now I'm retired."

"I'm a schoolteacher," continues his daughter. "I worked at the same school before the war, and then after the fighting when we returned from Zagreb. I got my job back. But life isn't easy now; my husband died three months ago."

"After everything that's happened in Jasenovac, why do you live here?"

"This is my home, our home," the old man asserts, his voice rising and trembling. "I have a right to my land. This is my land!" His daughter touches his arm to restrain him, mutters something soothingly. He doesn't look at her but obediently goes quiet, still trembling. Here is a man, I realize, who determines his home by the location of his land, rather than by his nation, to which he doesn't feel he belongs.

"We don't have anything to say about this," she adds.

"What's life like with the Croats now?"

"We don't have anything to say," she repeats, pressing his arm again.

"Do you spend time with them?"

"Very little," he says. "None really."

"You probably have Serb friends here, right?"

"Of course, of course."

"I guess I don't need to ask what you think of Croatia now," I ask, knowing there's nothing else I'll get from them.

"No point," she smiles sardonically. As we turn to go, she adds, "But that is statement enough in itself."

As we drive off, I think about Jasenovac's past. This past has become a focus of Croat and Serb political positions based on the numbers of victims, an index for foreign writers of Croat complicity and self-exoneration. It got Tudjman sent to prison for saying that in all the camps in Croatia during World War Two, only sixty thousand people lost their lives, not six hundred thousand; and not only Serbs and Jews but also Croats and others he called anti-fascists.

Tudjman visited Jasenovac on Bloomsday, June 16, 1996. In domestic political terms, he could afford to come after the Oluja (Storm) offensive the year before, which cleansed the Krajina region of Serbs in a blitzkrieg lasting a few days. His visit seemed magnanimous but was also meant for foreign consumption. Two years later, he had the former commander of Jasenovac put on trial in Zagreb. Dinko Šakić was sentenced to twenty years for crimes against humanity (yet not the more serious offence of genocide, some critics noted). He'd been living in Argentina since 1947 and was arrested there after a TV interview in which he incriminated himself by admitting to running the camp between 1942 and 1944, but humanely so that "not one guard or inmate was allowed to touch a prisoner."

On June 25, 1999, a large peasant demonstration began in Slavonia. Tens of thousands of peasants on their tractors and combines blocked highways and roads, including all the border crossings with Hungary. This situation was considerably different, however, from the one which produced the revolt of 1573. In 1999, there were no more serfs or Ottoman incursions; no one was crowned with molten iron or died in violent clashes, and very few Orthodox peasants were left in Krajina. The revolt took on the form of a common European demonstration. After five days, it was over, and the government agreed to the peasants' demands for more cash for wheat and protective tariffs on agricultural products.

The memory of Stjepan Radić (1871–1928) lies behind these ultimately peaceful events. Once the country's most powerful political figure, in 1904, Radić, along with his older brother Antun, founded the Croatian Popular Peasants Party—Croatia's strongest political force in the early twentieth century. During his summer vacation in 1886, he distinguished himself from the Slavonian peasantry into which he was born by setting off on a remarkable walking trip from Zagreb to Belgrade and back to his native district of Sisak. He kept a diary of what people thought about the government, the economic position of peasants, the state of roads, and other matters. He was enthused by the good treatment he received from both Croats and his "brother Serbs":[2]

> It was then that I decided never to be an official, but to devote myself entirely to defending the rights of the people and to their education. My father did not oppose my plans and my mother was delighted with them. She predicted that I would often be arrested, but this she did not mind, preferring it to my either being a lawyer or a priest, for, she said, lawyers must plead that falsehood is truth and truth falsehood, and the pocket of priests has no bottom.[3]

Nine years later, in 1895, Radić embarked on a more politically charged journey around Croatia, this time by train. He wanted to show that the Nagodba agreement signed with the Hungarians, which guaranteed Croatian administrative autonomy, had been broken through the use of Hungarian on-the-state railway. He also wanted to prove that the railways entrenched the Hungarian policy of suppressing Croatia and undermining Austrian commerce, since all goods had to be transported through Hungarian-controlled Rijeka on the coast or Budapest.

> Wherever he went, he asked for information in Croatian, demanded that his ticket be printed in Croatian as well as Hungarian and would only speak Croatian to the conductors even though most of them were Hungarians. In a series of articles for the main opposition newspaper, *Obzor* (Horizon), Radić described his adventures on the network and in particular the abuse and threats levelled at him by the staff. His odyssey culminated in a dramatic attempt by Hungarian railway workers to throw him off a speeding train.[4]

Later that same year, Radić was imprisoned for six months for leading students in a Hungarian flag-burning at Jelačić Square.

Ultimately, he distinguished himself from more extreme politicians because he compromised with the hated Karadjordjević dynasty in Serbia—which controlled the Kingdom of Serbs, Croats, and Slovenes—in order to achieve good educational and living standards for all peasants, not just Croats. After a period of resistance to Belgrade, during which he was tossed into prison a few times, Radić made an abrupt about-face and served as the Minister of Education. Still, he continued his more accustomed role of lambasting the federal government. This stance made him dangerous, maybe more so than his ethnicity. But when he was shot on June 19, 1928 in the Belgrade Parliament during a vitriolic session rife with nationalist fury, it was because he was a Croat. A Montenegrin Serb gunned him down along with other members of the HSS, including Radić's nephew, who took a bullet to save him. Surviving for nearly two months, Radić eventually died on August 8 and was given a funeral reserved for heads of state or royalty. One hundred thousand people proceeded through Zagreb's streets. His murderer was put under house arrest but never tried.

Immediately after the shootings, riots and general unrest began in earnest in Croatia, resulting in hundreds of injuries and deaths. King Alexander Karadjordjević shut down democratic rule on January 6, 1929, abolishing the constitution, parliament, and political parties, and renaming the country the Kingdom of Yugoslavia. For many Croats, these actions resulted in a notorious dictatorship. It might be argued that the so-called endemic hatred between Croats and Serbs hardened then—especially since in preceding years, popular movements were afoot to unite the two groups, not split them.

Sixty-three years later, the murdering began again. This time it originated in the industrial Vukovar suburb of Borovo Selo in eastern Slavonia and didn't let up for four years. On May 1, 1991, two young Croat policeman were kidnapped and killed by Serb villagers. Twelve more were killed the next day during the attempt to reclaim the bodies. The Croat media alleged that some of the policemen were mutilated, a few while they were still alive. The first two policemen apparently intended to replace the town hall's Yugoslav flag with the new Croatian *šahovnica*. This act echoes one that took place in an earlier era of rising Croat nationalism in Zaprešić, a village west of Zagreb. The year was 1903 and the Hungarian army fired on peasants "taking a flag down from the railway station, and this led to new disorders through almost all of Civil Croatia. Peasants went on the rampage and broke the windows of hated *Magyarones*, threw Hungarian officials out of their offices, and burned portraits of [*ban*] Héderváry and Hungarian flags."[5]

Borovo Selo became memorable, not because it was unique in the wars that erupted throughout the former Yugoslavia, but because it was the first incontrovertible sign that an appalling line had been crossed: that things could come to this, spiral out of control, go to extremes—that the country had suffered a brutalization. It became evident to Croats, if not the entire western world, that Borovo Selo marked a sudden upsurge in the Serb military presence in the area, along with Yugoslav army support. The howitzers were being loaded.

In order to engage the Serbs militarily, Croatian cabinet minister Gojko Šušak and his extreme nationalist henchmen in the Vukovar region felt they needed, among other things, to get rid of a regional Croat police chief, Josip Reihl-Kir.[6] The problem was that Reihl-Kir wanted peace. He would appear at barricades to calm the sides, sometimes convincing them to clear the roads and go home. He would show up unarmed, opening his jacket as a first step of his negotiations. His predictable, non-violent approach was initially the key to his success. But he was working in an increasingly militant environment in which being a peacenik, from the Croat perspective, was more and more tantamount to being pro-Serb. From the Serb perspective, such a stance was more and more irrelevant and annoying, given their military superiority at the time and their objectives in Slavonia.

Reihl-Kir knew he was in danger. He went to Zagreb to ask Police Minister Josip Boljkovac to transfer him. He accused Šušak and his entourage, led by local HDZ man Branimir Glavaš, of planning to kill him. "Please, save me. I know the situation here very well. I am going to lose my life. We are losing control down here."[7] The police chief was to be moved on July 2, but he went to one last Croat checkpoint to defuse another situation. This time his predictability undid him. On July 1, one of his own subordinates walked up and shot him dead. Anton Gudelj was a young Croat officer who'd just been told that the

Serbs had killed most of his family, and he was in a psychotic frame of mind. Ironically, Gudelj used the very Kalshnikov he'd requested from Reihl-Kir a few days earlier.

Vukovar was next. The Serbs attacked in the fall of 1991, employing heavy weapons, tanks, and air power against a small, lightly armed band of around two thousand defenders. Miraculously, despite Tudjman's tacit consent to Vukovar's defeat—he hoped to acquire international respectability by agreeing to "internationally brokered ceasefires"[8]—the battle lasted for nearly three months. As a result, Vukovar has become one of the most important symbols of Croat resistance to Serb aggression, even though (or perhaps because) the city fell on November 18, 1991.

The Serbs won nothing. Vukovar was a hellish wasteland, a vast sector of rubble. Brutally destroyed, it spoke powerfully of hate, cowardice, evil, brutality, immorality, influence at the highest levels, despair, sacrifice, and bravery. Vukovar changed in status, and its past became more important to Croats than ever. It became important to know its history, both the interesting and the mundane—that its location on the Danube made it a stop for steamships in the mid nineteenth century and a big reloading port, that it boasted the 1939 Nobel Laureate in chemistry, Lavoslav Ruzička, and that it was once home to a BATA rubber and shoe factory as well as a Turkish military centre in the sixteenth century.

Pondering Vukovar's destruction makes me hopeful that the memories of people like Reihl-Kir will endure. I recall the storks in Jasenovac. By returning to towns from which they were driven away by war, they are telling us that it's a good time to build anew, a good time to live. But for how long, I wonder. Places in Slavonia seem haunted with souls gone too soon, unabsolved, awaiting a reckoning.

6 ■ THE KVARNER ISLANDS
Krk, Rab

UNLIKE FLAT, AGRICULTURAL SLAVONIA, CROATIA'S Adriatic coast is rocky and Mediterranean in character. Nothing adequately prepares travellers for this contrast of regions, this departure from the base, all-too-human land of the interior for the land of gods. Indeed, this area seems inhospitable to human life, and only sunshine pearling off the white islands can transform their barren ruthlessness. Yet the islands and the sea are a beautiful sight at the end of the road through mountainous and forested Gorski Kotar, showing up unannounced through a blue haze. I feel as if I've climbed out of an abyss and seen the view from the top of the world.

The bridge from the mainland to the island takes me to the small town of Omišalj. Because it is still early in the day, my legs have energy to spare and my backpack feels light. I wander around, unrestricted by my watch, which is somewhere in my pack. From a terrace by the Romanesque church of Sveti Antun, a view opens onto Istria's Učka Mountains on the right. Someone is playing piano in a large, elegant house. The front door and windows are open, as if to share the music, and curtains blow in and out, waving a greeting. I listen for a while in peace.

Omišalj is the site of the August harvest festival, Stomorina, when troupes dress in bright costumes similar to those at Krapina's festival, perform local dances, and sing songs like "Turne Moj Lipi" ("My Beautiful Tower"), which Ivan Frankopan allegedly sang when he was sent packing by the Venetians at the request of his own subjects. He was the last Frankopan Count of Krk, one of a dynasty that governed the island under the nominal rule of Hungary-Croatia and Venice from the twelfth to fifteenth centuries. As Rebecca West notes, they were "typical Dalmatian nobles: of unknown origin, probably aliens who had come down on the Slavs when they were exhausted by barbarian invasions, and who were themselves of barbarian blood. Certainly they owed their ascendancy not to virtue or to superior culture, but to unusual steadfastness in seeing that it was always the other man who was beheaded or tossed from the window or smothered."[1] In Ivan Frankopan, generations of paranoia and political tightroping over the chasm between empires coalesced in a megalo-mania as fevered as any in world history. He even turned against all eight of his younger brothers, making Venice heir to his possessions as a means of self-protection. "He conceived the idea that he must have an infinite amount of money to save him from disaster; he robbed his peasants of their last coins, and murdered refugees who landed on his island, in flight from the Turk, for the sake of their little stores."

I leave town and walk east. Deciduous trees spread their shade along the edges of the road, which climbs and descends in easy swells like the path of a boat on the waves. This side of the island isn't far enough off the coast to have that spare elemental quality of the Adriatic. But an island it is, the biggest in Croatia and the only one with a river. It's considered a cradle of Croatian language and literacy, where the Glagolitic alphabet was fostered after having been intro-duced by followers of Greek missionaries Cyril and Methodius for the Slavic liturgy. (Glagolitic is from *glagol*, common Slavonic for "word.") The Bašćanska Ploča (Baška Tablet) is one of the oldest written docu-ments in this alphabet, and while it's housed in Zagreb, many other Glagolitic documents are preserved across the island, especially in the fortified town of Vrbnik.

I come to Krk town in the heat and hazy dustiness. Stray pieces of paper are cycloning in the corners of the deserted square. On my right is a large cathedral with an onion-domed tower, Uznesenje Marijino, and on my left is the Frankopans' roofless fortified castle (1191). On one of the large wooden cathedral doors is a yellow stone carving of a hand, palm out, its first two fingers pointing skyward in what looks like a peace sign but makes me think of the greater power above.

Through a narrow, arched corridor tiled like a chessboard, I exit the town and arrive at the harbour promenade. The sun's heat feels like an oven blast, but once I'm further along it cools as a breeze blows off the water. I spot my first human, a middle-aged guy in a white undershirt, jeans, and thongs, sitting on a bench under pine trees. A big beer beside him, he's in a stupor, contemplating three skiffs on workhorses. They look ready to be painted. *Now how should I go about doing this*, he's thinking, *and when should I start what with this heat? Better wait until later, finish this up first.*

"I tell ya, my son," he says. "I don't know where that lazy kid a mine's to, but he's got a job later. He can chase them cunts some other time. All this, my son, see?" he complains, waving his arm at the boats. Were he in a better mood, he would sing the beautiful old tune "And Those Masts":

> Those are not masts of my boat, but those are the legs
> of my Marica.
> Those are not oars of my boat, but those are the arms
> of my Marica.
> Those are not sails of my boat, but those are the
> panties of my Marica.
> *Čiri biri bela Mare moja, čiri biri bela Mare moja....*

I find a room for the night through the travel agency, and after resting for a few hours, I return to town. The place has come to life as people have emerged from their cool stone houses to do their business or socialize. The fisherman is painting Milano red stripes along the skiffs' sides and a kid of around sixteen is lethargically painting the propellers

A cobbled street in Krk, 1996.

black. Similar skiffs in the water are prepared for a night run, nets folded inside and lanterns screwed on. No one else is working this evening. Young women wearing freshly minted faces walk through the streets arm in arm and gangs of muscled young men sit on their motorbikes. Age-old rites of courtship go on as always. Like elsewhere on the Adriatic and throughout the Mediterranean, socializing in the squares, streets, and quays is entrenched in the culture. Even though many towns and villages can't be termed cities, many are unmistakably urban. They seem designed to facilitate meetings between people and satisfy a way of daily living in a community.

I take a brief tour through Krk's stone innards. Smooth flagstones glisten from the setting sun that slants into the empty streets. I smell lamb meat through one open window, and hear shouts in the distance. My legs are tiring. I struggle back to my room and lie gratefully down for the night, ready to wake early for the trip to Baška and the ferry to Rab.

■

The next morning a taxi takes me on a new highway by the sea, then inland. Cream-coloured walls, olive groves, and maquis make this side of Krk more typically Adriatic, giving the island a split personality. We climb to the peak then descend steeply between mountains to Baška. The town is positioned on a small bay in the cramped space between the surrounding mountains. Without Krk's fortifications, less sculptured and massive, it's a pretty, yet dilapidated, place. Some of the houses dating back to the sixteenth century have chimneys that are extra-fortified against the wintry blasts of the Bura that blows strongest through the mountains at the coastal town of Senj.

I experienced the Bura once up close when I was younger. As my parents and I drove to the resort of Tučepi, the Bura hurricaned across the highway, swaying our Citroën. Being blown off a cliff and down the terrifying chasm to the sea seemed realistically possible, so we stopped at a roadhouse. I remember feeling light, fragile, flying off my dad's hand like a kite. In retrospect, I doubt the wisdom of stepping out of a car that weighed considerably more than we did and into winds that can clock 120 kilometres per hour.

Today is windless. I manage to buy a ticket in time and get on the ferry. It sails through the slender sea corridor called the Senjska Vrata (doors of Senj), where ships used to flounder regularly—and not only because of the Bura.

In the sixteenth and seventeenth centuries, Senj used to be the base for the infamous Uskok pirates and bandits who plundered Venetian and Ottoman ships, raiding and murdering for booty throughout the interior border world where the Hapsburg monarchy, the Republic of Venice, and the Ottoman Empire collided. From *uskočiti* (to jump in), the Uskoci were essentially Croat refugees fleeing the westward advances of the Ottomans, although some were Muslims and Orthodox

Vlachs (pastoral nomads who eventually came to identify themselves as Serbs). Mainly they were Senj natives, Croats from Hapsburg territory, Dalmatians under Venetian rule, and citizens of the Republic of Ragusa (as Dubrovnik used to be called). The Uskoci operated loosely under the auspices of Hapsburg monarchy from the early 1500s until roughly 1617, when the Hapsburgs agreed to Venetian demands to disband them, at least around Senj.

In *The Uskoks of Senj*, Catherine Wendy Bracewell problematizes the simple perception of Uskoci as either murderous thugs or soldiers on the ramparts of Christianity who saved Europe from the darkness of Islam. Uskok identity depends on who characterizes them. The Venetians and Ottomans sought to destroy the Uskoci, since they severely hindered trade. In contrast, the Hapsburgs tolerated and even encouraged them, incorporating them into the workings of their military frontier. Croat peasants immortalized the Uskoci in songs, even though many peasants suffered brutally from the bandits' raids. As for the Uskoci themselves, they seemed to have legitimized themselves as Christian crusaders with a fearsome code of honour, which included the sanctity of their word, loyalty to their people, and such unchristian things as swift vengeance against enemies, courage in fighting, pride in battle wounds, and acquisition of trophies (like money, slaves, livestock, decapitated heads, and cut-off noses). While one wonders about the religious integrity of the Uskoci, local friars appear to have supported their cause:

> One of these, Fra Simon Urmaneo, had gone from house to house visiting those who were reluctant to join the Uskoci and rebels, bearing a distaff and a spindle and saying, "Take this, sluggard, put down your arquebus and sword and takes these as your arms. These are the exercises that suit you. Put on a woman's dress and stay at home spinning in shame. Don't you see that your contemporaries are at war and are fighting for the faith."[2]

The Uskok mentality has lasted to this day. Theirs is a border gestalt, a mode of survival and strategy of conquest based on aggression.

The rooftops of Rab, 1996.

It was exhibited by extremist Serbs in Krajina who felt threatened by Croatia's new regime in the 1990s, and further south by extremist Croats of Herzegovina. Indeed, the Uskoci have become Croat heroes, standing for the struggle of lightly armed Davids against imperialist Goliaths, the siege of Vukovar being the latest theatre for this drama.[3]

"Mister," the old man says from his seat at a café outside the town of Rab, "that is one long road." His face is creased like leather and his blue eyes are swimming with *šljivovica*. Waving me up the concrete steps to the seat across from him, he calls over the café owner, a paunchy guy laden with gold chains and rings and wearing a big-collared, flowery shirt. He brings three brimming shot glasses and we knock them in a toast and down the burning stuff. It hits me like a hot hand that reaches warm fingers inside my chest, around my lungs and my heart.

The old man wags a thick finger, "This is the most beautiful island in all of Croatia. You got a lot to see." Looking at the town of Rab across the bay—a shimmering prow of white walls jutting into the sea, with four slender steeples like masts rising from the fray of orange-tiled roofs—I can't imagine he's wrong. This panorama is the most striking scene for any traveller to Rab.

At home I have a black-and-white postcard of the same view, the only memento of my German grandmother's trip here in 1938. Her short pencilled greeting to her family in Kiel, in her spidery German writing, is still as clear as the day it was written. "Hello to all of you, my family. Leni," was all she wrote. She was a young woman, only thirty-five then. A strange charge ghosts through me when I imagine her eyes panning across these same walls, as if we'd suddenly met in the space of some long-forgotten wish image of hers.

That charge is like the sun, a flashy coin in the bright blue, like I'm ambling down the harbour promenade into the palm-treed square, where fruit and vegetable merchants sit listlessly in the shade and young trinket peddlers unfold their displays for the evening. This is the end of the hot dream time, the afternoon's siesta hours, when a sluggish, windless air still hangs over the town.

... *An old woman dressed in black from head to foot hawks sea-shells and starfish in the shade of a palm tree. Her face is pale grey, her hands large and rough. A small knee-high table is loaded with her things. Coming closer, I notice a large sand dollar with a faded picture of the seaside and the red letters* Schleswig Holstein. *The charge is torquing inside my brain when I read those words, as the fisherwoman explains in her rasping dialect, in a voice like a traveller coming from a distant place, that she knows me, indeed has been waiting so long to pass this on to me.*

■

In 1988, when I first arrived from the mainland settlement of Jablanac on one of Croatia's Jadrolinija car ferries, I was shocked and disappointed by the desolate, white, rocky surface of the island. Under a blue sky raked by seagulls riding the wind currents, wind snapping the ship's flags to attention and tearing the water into white rags, Rab reared up like some huge reptile encased in cracked, crumbling scales. Nothing here seemed worth coming for.

No sooner was I away from the dock than I saw the country transform. But unlike Pag, it becomes a rich garden with dusty juniper, olive, and fig orchards, low-growing vineyards, neatly parcelled corn plots, and wood and wire pens containing goats and sheep. Uncultivated stone-pocked fields are sprinkled with thyme, rosemary, and a yellow herb with a curry aroma, which one peasant woman told me was *bosilje*, a form of basil.

On a paved road winding up from the sea, then along a baked brick-hard path like one of hundreds criss-crossing the island, I make my way towards an abandoned turn-of-the-century house. The balustrades on its two spacious balconies show the residual signs of Italian influence on Rab. This house seems squarely locked in that distant time, standing here like an incongruity among the empty fields and farmhouses and modern villas. It has a monumental quality; it is three storeys tall with a central pilaster, iron-adorned wooden doors, and a walled granite terrace.

But the house is falling to pieces. Ceramic roof tiles lie shattered on the terrace, the doors have rusted off the hinges, and the eastern balcony slopes dangerously towards the terrace. Inside, the walls are cracked, the floorboards decayed or missing and the steps warped and frail. Signs of the house's reversion to the natural world are everywhere: bird droppings on the windowsills, a wasp's nest in one corner, spiders' webs in the others, and weeds growing through cracks in the floor.

Still, an aura of humanity haunts the house. This mood is the equivalent of a blurred daguerreotype, as if the accumulated density of the movements and conversations and dreams and hatreds and loves of the people once living here hazes the air, between the still and silent walls. Someone stood in this hall and walked up these stairs and leaned out these windows. Things happened in rooms here and here and here, at night, in whispers—things never to be known and forever lost. All that's left are a few abandoned bits of evidence: that laceless boot still crusted with dirt from some muddy winter walk, this rusty pot left upstairs for some reason, and, astonishingly, letters, postcards, receipts, and pages from newspapers. "Dear Papa," one letter from 1928 reads, "Everyone is healthy here and we hope you are well too." How grounded and simple this wish is, so incompatible with the house's aristocratic pretensions.

There is one story. The renegade twin brother now living in Serbia refuses to sell or hand over this property to his dead twin's family. Instead, he lets the place fall apart. When he dies, the property will pass on to his children in Belgrade. Maybe they will relent after he's gone, if indeed they actually exist.

I like to mull this story over, but no more than that. Searching out the facts would disturb these haunts for me and unwind the coiled history that twists through these islands like the cobblestone streets through town, complex and cryptic. Everywhere I look, there are pieces of stories never put together—puzzles to solve, never to be solved. Such unexplained gaps are most interesting to me, as if personal histories were never written here, only happening unceremoniously and usually lost. This place has always belonged to its present, its meaning forever locked up to its future like a mute bursting with secrets.

Nevertheless, personal memories do exist and some are passed on. These words appeared in the guest book of the Imperial Hotel:

> The white-walled town by the blue Adriatic lived on as
> a pale image in my memory, a shimmer of orange roofs,
> steeples and narrow streets, hidden beyond broken
> coastline and stony hills, like gold in a prospector's pan.
>
> This is how I remember Rab, where I first saw the light
> of day. A vision on long trips, in bars when time was
> like all the worthless coins in my pockets.
>
> After years away, I stood on a steamboat impatiently
> waiting to see the steeples again. Then I had another
> vision of the old town. White buildings of a new world
> lay on the ruins of the old, young people speaking

unfamiliar languages roamed the streets, strange music from far away countries played in the cafés. I walked around amazed, like a beggar invited to a feast.

But on my way into the oldest part of Rab, the sounds receding in the distance, the streets leading me back to the dark unwritten periods of the town's history, I felt cold in my bones. Walking on the Latin-inscribed tombs of long-dead monks and in the steps of unknown people who wore these stones smooth, I felt the ghosts of the old world sweep past me and heard the bells toll their memory.

■

"Listen," says the old man at the café, touching my shoulder. "The fuckers running things now are ruining everything. We had something before and tourists used to come. But everyone's afraid now because of the war."

Two men join us. The young one has a brush cut, bleached blond from the sun, and blue eyes as bright as my host's. The old one is fat and bare-chested, with a doughy, pockmarked face. My host, called Ivo, introduces me and we shake hands all around. Brush Cut tells the owner to serve us some more shots and I reluctantly agree, although I actually like the buzz they're giving me.

Brush Cut, or Johnny as he's known, finished one year toward an engineering degree at the University of Zagreb, but quit to run his dad's fishing and tour boat operation. There's cynicism in his words and demeanour as he describes the poor economic and political situation in his country. I wonder how much he regrets coming back to Rab, R.E.M.'s "Don't Go Back to Rockville" popping into my head. But Rab is no Rockville and Johnny no angst-ridden North American kid with a superiority complex. He's bitter but in a constructive way, unwilling to let bad times take over his life. "Tito held us in his iron hand, but he had a direction. People liked him. They put his name in stones," he says, referring to the massive assembly of white rocks near the summit of hills outside town.

"Tito was the son of a whore, a killer like Stalin," the fat man suddenly says.

"There he goes again," says Ivo and bangs his hand on the table. "Look piggy, quit scratchin' yourself and pay attention. You got tits as big as my wife's and brains just as small."

"He was a murderer. Took my brother away."

"Oh fuck, here he goes," Ivo's voice trails off as if he's beaten and has no rejoinder. Such is the paradox of Tito's legacy, that even his supporters can be silenced by the human cost of his iron hand.

A young man swaggers up to the café steps and leans on the railing. His brown hair is shaved, his grey-blue eyes slyly watching us. He smirks when they give him a cheer. He's a former volunteer soldier in the Croat army who fought in Vukovar. No one mentions Tito now. This is what he tells me, speaking respectfully because he appreciates my coming, but forcefully as if he couldn't care less what I think. "When I held my gun the first time, my heart was this big," he says, his hands spanning twice his body width. "And I knew I was a man."

A fraction of silence follows. If I feel anything in this moment, it's a fleeting sense of their weighing his statement, a split-second attempt to separate the seriousness of his words from the fanaticism. Then Ivo retorts, "Sure, a man's man." And everyone laughs, and the soldier laughs.

It's morning. The sun is well up and already blazing, but in the shady streets and in the pine forest above town the air is crisp and cool. It's silent now except for the voices of a few locals in cafés, in the markets, and on the piers, the tourists blessedly not here yet.

Leaving a good place always makes me try to memorize every sight, sound, and smell, the totality of my experience, the emotional resonance—maybe because I feel I won't ever be back. I take my time on my way up to Slobode Square, with its view of the bell towers and the monastery of St. Antun Opata and the narrow arm of the St. Eufemija channel. For me, Rab appears unmistakably foreign with its beautiful hybrid architecture, not all of it consigned to historical oblivion. A few places come to mind: the harbour's Knežev Dvor (Prince's Palace), with its thirteenth-century Romanesque tower, and the large Renaissance palace exhibiting the coat of arms of the Christian Ninimir and Dominis families. The latter is the birthplace of Mark Antun Dominis (1560–1624), Dean of Windsor under King James, a Jesuit scholar and scientist whose work on the spectrum was recognized by Newton, and who first proved the moon's influence on the tides.[4]

When I reach the square, I see the islands in the blue distance, dotting the Adriatic. I see the narrow stone promenade bordering the channel from which some swimmers slip into the still mirror-like water, split here and there by sailboats. The steps and the promenade are wet with morning dew, the sun not yet high enough over the town to shine here. I thread my way between some large stones and slide into the cool, dark water. Two hundred metres into the channel and looking back, Rab is a dark, long jewel fringed by sun fire that slowly creeps across its roofs, an eruption of civilization in a scorched stone world.

7  POVLJANA
The Sea Stars

THE STRETCH OF HIGHWAY SOUTH OF PAG CUTS
through a wide valley bordered by white hills where broken stone
churches and farmhouses sit like forgotten miracles of handicraft and
sheer will. I head to the village of Povljana after leaving Pag town
behind—that charming grid of flagstoned streets and multicoloured
buildings, lime and yellow and white.

It's another hot morning on a baking slab of concrete. My canvas
backpack, shut with a safety pin, is sweating up my back. This isn't
the first time I've regretted my ambition to walk down the Adriatic
coast. But so far, so good; the road is flat and straight, a light north
wind provides extra coolness, and long puffy clouds majestically sail
under the sun like aircraft carriers. I hide inside the shadows that slide
across the earth in steady battalions. Soft bleatings of sheep blow in
from the fields.

On my right are squares of water, like rice paddies, divided by
knee-high wood fences; these are the salt pans of Pag, which produce
salt in backwater stores across Croatia. Further along, a shadowy
monstrosity looms beside the road like a blue metallic triceratops—a

plated and hinged reminder of archaic industry, like some vestige of nineteenth-century industrial England shipped here and assembled. The salt factory looks abandoned, a structure that's just *there*, a phenomenon of nature that can't explain its own existence.

Soon after, a yellow sign points me to the right. The slender road descends sharply and brings me into flat, stone-pocked land, with fields of sparse grass stretching all the way to the sea, marked off by the same hip-high rock walls that hold down the whole island. Cadaverous sheep are huddled near the road in the narrow shade of a wall, waiting out the sun's passage across the sky. A hut, roofed with the same rough white blocks as the walls and with small rectangular windows like gunsights, stands in the empty field as a monument, a sign of that effort to found a human presence in this ungiving place. It reminds me of abandoned prairie farmhouses and their rusted machinery lodged in the earth, overgrown with grass.

I have the empty feeling of going nowhere. No birds have taken to wing and no sounds are travelling on the wind now; even the clouds have escaped to the south, baring the naked sky. But I'm at peace, and in the middle of this sparse world I find small things to interest me: geckos scurry off their sunning spots, black and grey stippled snakes whip their tails at me and escape my thundering steps, and the fields are sprinkled with barbed *čičak* thistle, which will soon blush blue at the tips as it does every summer.

In a small field enclosed by a thicket of acacia and olive trees, a white Clydesdale is dragging a plow through the dry earth. When I take a picture, one of the two farmers shakes a fist and shouts at me, "Boy, I'm coming over there to take your film. You never got my permission." I stop, stuck in my tracks. I wait for him to come over, but the men laugh and continue working. The guy waves, so I wave back and leave them to carve and saw the earth, their shouts fading behind me.

I'm alone once more, in flat terrain pried apart from a sky so high and thinly blue that it seems to be dissipating altogether, soon to show the star-sprinkled night behind it, the black universe. For a while there are no sounds.

A rumble comes from the direction of the highway, and I see something glinting in the pavement heat. The pipes are long and polished bright, the teardrop tanks pearl white, and the spokes a bright, silvery whir. Three Harley-style Yamahas with Croat plates cruise past, driven by two men and a woman sheathed in cracked black leather, like Hell's Angels from some B-movie. As they roll slowly past, one of the men flicks his head at the seat behind him. As if we were supposed to meet here all along, I hop on without breaking stride. A smell of sweat, cigarettes, and liquor wafts from under his tight jacket, the back of which bears a big *šahovnica*.

He points to his left saddlebag and shouts in English, "Have some Jack." I pull out a mickey of Jack Daniel's and shakily use both hands to twist off the cap. I take a slug of some pristine fiery liquid. "*Viljamovka*," he says, motioning for the bottle. I remember the orchards in the hills south of Zagreb, where bottles hang from pear trees, twinkling in the sun. They are hung each spring so that the mature pears, eventually imprisoned by glass, will decorate the pear brandy poured inside. *Viljamovka*. After a couple of shots, he tucks the bottle between his legs and drives on to Povljana.

We stop at a tiny, posh café on what looks like a main street of this quiet village. Some good-looking young men, nicely coiffed, wearing T-shirts, black jeans, and sandals, are smoking and drinking beer. Looking narrowly at us, they go on talking like they've seen our kind a dozen times over.

When I say goodbye to my driver, he tosses me the *viljamovka* and tells me it's "something for company." I lift it in thanks and make my way down the street toward the wedge of blue sky and sea that is partly blocked from view by villas and houses. Doors are open, fruit, vegetables, and weigh scales sit on the cement walls, but there's not a person in sight, not a soul moving. I've wandered into an Adriatic Sleepy Hollow where everything's in slow motion; a thick wind sluggishly sways the trees, swallows tilt overhead like lethargic seagulls, and hummingbirds flutter inelegantly above flowers like butterflies. A fishing boat sits frozen near the horizon, and flags on the skiffs and ships at dock furl and unfurl like arthritic hands, opening and closing. From the docks I see the little bay and peninsula in the distance—a long, rocky finger dusted by grass and thatched with pines. Rock walls zigzag over the top and down the other side, and just above the main beach stands a tiny stone chapel, built around the tenth century and surrounded by a cemetery grown over with tall grass, its crosses leaning left and right.

The boats bobbing slowly up and down make the water gurgle sleepily, so I drop my pack and lie down. I'm tired—hungry, too. The booze is singing nicely in my head. Eyes shut against the sun's glare and the sharp sky, I listen to the mantra of sea sounds around me.

She's ten yards away when I open my eyes again, padding towards me. Wild blonde curls frame a tanned face with jade eyes that see coldly past me. She walks to the tip of the dock, strips to her white bikini, and dives neatly into the water. After climbing the little steps back onto the dock, she dives in again. Emerging, she dries her hair with her hands, her face turned up to the sun.

I address her in English, figuring this will somehow intrigue her. "Nice day, eh?" I begin, sounding to myself like an American parody of a Canadian. On her back now, she turns her head languidly in my direction, looking at me or through me. "How's the water?" I try again. She brushes drops off her brown belly and closes her eyes.

It must be me. I pick up my pack and walk back up the road. The pine forest sighs coded messages to seagulls whirling around the treetops. Motionless, the boat on the horizon seems forever delayed on its way home.

■

The world accelerates as swallows dart by and leaves flicker brightly like tossed coins or fountain spray. A fat woman in a white kerchief and apron sits on her cement veranda, peeling potatoes. I notice a naked foot poking out of an open balcony door. Povljana in the afternoon is very quiet, only disturbed in my earshot by rumbles from my stomach.

A balding young waiter, neatly dressed in pressed white shirt and navy slacks, brings me a menu at one of Povljana's restaurants. Like most of the people I've met, he's pleased I've come all this way to see his country, but incredulous that I planned to walk all the way down. "This is a new country, yes," he says in English, "but you know we have big buses, ferries too." He smiles, partly condescending to what he perceives as foreign ignorance and partly agitated by it. His feelings belong to a complex nationalistic pride that takes different forms, sometimes chauvinistic and militaristic, sometimes social and cultural, often a combination of the two. He's not a zealot but he seems to regard Croatia as a young Switzerland needing only proper planning or care, like a garden that must be tended in order for its full potential to be realized. As he talks, he keeps looking over my shoulder at potential customers passing by.

I tell him I see more travelling this way, and I meet more people. "I'm a writer, see," I explain, pulling out my ratty notebook.

"Not everything bullets and death, I hope," he says. "That's what these foreign journalists like to write." He seems contemptuous about outside, imperialistic influences. Forty-six years of Yugoslav socialism won't be erased overnight. However, Croats like him often betray a decidedly bourgeois attitude when it comes to the power of their money, hungering for the standard of living they've seen first-hand elsewhere. They'll condemn the salesman but buy his products. Yet my waiter isn't entirely satisfied with the way things are going in Croatia. He tells me his father was fired as Povljana's tourist coordinator after Croatia's self-declared independence. I don't know if this means that his father was an especially strident communist—many people declared themselves communists as a method of self-promotion—but his firing seemed politically motivated, a purging of the old communist guard.

Such thoughts only flash momentarily through my mind, because my stomach has taken over. My waiter brings me an order of *ražnjići*, pork shish kebabs on wooden skewers served with fries, diced onions, and a dab of *ajvar*, a spicy sauce that is Macedonian in origin and made of tomato, onion, and eggplant. As a gesture of goodwill and business savvy, he offers me a glass of his father's homemade *loza*.

After finishing, I jot a few observations in my notebook, breaking away now and then to gaze through the gap between the fig trees at the villas and the bay. A footpath winds through little parcels of farmers' fields and gardens to a paved road that turns towards the beach. Only the hot, whispering wind and a rare donkey's bray disturbs this siesta silence. As I walk down to the sea, bees are humming in the little fields, and finches are swooping in flocks from fig tree to fig tree. A radiant sun hangs over the pine-thatched peninsula. Lined with silent villas, the road becomes a short stretch of gravel curving beside

Sveti Nikola chapel in Povljana, 1997.

a newly mowed field and Sveti Nikola chapel. What a beautiful, peaceful place. If I have to die, let it be here—poppies in the cemetery dancing in the wind, a turquoise sea behind.

In the shadowy green depths, dark fish are swimming casually, and on the sea floor are hundreds of sea cucumbers. I front-crawl towards the cement mooring in the harbour, five hundred yards away. As elsewhere on the coast this time of year, there are no waves to speak of and I soon arrive, hauling myself up by one of the rusted rings.

The girl is gone. An old woman in a pink bathing cap has taken her place, so for a second I feel like Rip Van Winkle, who slept his life away. I do a few cannonballs off the block, then doze awhile on top. On the way back, I fancy that the villas I remembered here and there have disappeared, that the electrical lines I swear were connected to the last house under the peninsula are gone. For a minute I'm convinced Povljana has returned to some moment in its past, before it existed in my consciousness, or that my very eyes and gaze now belong to someone else who came before me. These doppelgänger moments must be expressions of a solitary brain wandering in a foreign place. It's not the first time I've felt a secret-sharer inside my skin peering out. When I return to the beach, the feelings go away because everything looks the same; my clothes are where I left them, and that stone stuck in the sand is the way I remember it. The only visible difference is a pair of wine barrels propped on an outcropping of brown rocks, set there in my absence to air out.

Before taking the road back, I visit the chapel. The walkway is made of stone slabs run together, tilting with the earth. A few of them look like sarcophagi carved with unreadable inscriptions. The front door with its steel lock looks like it was put there ten or fifteen years ago. A slit of a window on the western side, through which the sun now shines, offers a view into a round interior: a small altar and a wooden crucifix, a rickety dais with a half-melted candle, and three wooden benches. A swallow's nest is tucked into a corner on the altar's side, and cobwebs hang everywhere else. The chapel is spooky, making me wonder what people felt when they crowded inside—neighbours forced side by side in this little house of God.

On the road back towards the village, I realize that some of Povljana's streets meander to the country or sea like aimless cracks in a wall. There's no centre here, but instead many informal spaces at street crossings and elsewhere where people meet by happenstance and the ties of community hold. How different this village is compared to those in the north, where the linear configuration doesn't encourage daily get-togethers and peasants aren't in the habit of going out for evening chats or strolls. I think I could enjoy life here too. I try to imagine the slow pace of my days, the long winter hours playing cards in cafés, the boredom, friends as familiar to me as my skin, the gossip. Could I adjust to it all, I wonder. The Canadian in me, used to wide tracts of space and not knowing the first thing about my suburban neighbour, is probably too deeply ingrained. Where you come from often determines whether you can adjust to a place, no matter how much you want to live there.

Still, everything I see here makes me wish it were otherwise, mundane though these sights might be to locals. A farmer drives by on a tiny one-man tractor, its handlebars extending Harley-like from the engine. A herd of sheep presses me to the side. Two or three are

Old women after church in Povljana, 1997.

wearing bells, and in the middle of the herd is a single black back. A tired shepherd wearing a Chicago Bulls cap is swearing steadily, whacking stragglers with a branch. A sign of what their future holds, two bloody sheepskins, turned inside-out, hang from a fig tree.

I get a room in a private house for the night and shower outside in my bathing suit. A day's summer sunshine provides about five minutes of warm water from the black tank, though I hardly need it on an evening as warm as this one. Thinking I'm alone, I dry off and change into the cleanest pair of shorts I can find. But when I turn around, I see a very old woman dressed in black from kerchief to shoes, leaning her elbows on the wall and watching me peacefully—the way she might watch something familiar like chickens feeding, yet more interested than that. Her face looks like a dark brown saddle and her witch's nose hooks sharply towards her thin mouth. When she notices me noticing her, she pretends to find something interesting to her right, then sighs and hobbles back into her yard. It's only when I gather my stuff that I see my bottle of *viljamovka*, in the middle of the table like Wallace Stevens' jar in Tennessee.

At ten o'clock on a Saturday night, with my supper of *cevapčići* (paprika-spiced sausages) finished and a half-litre of beer pearling a tall glass, I sit back and stretch out my tired, sunburned legs. A fat German couple and their toy poodle are the other guests. From the bar, music pours out into the crisp star-filled night. Sleep is starting to sedate me.

Two of the guys from the café this afternoon arrive. Maybe eighteen or nineteen, they have style and a taste for the outside world. They give me the impression of wanting to belong anywhere except Povljana, but while they can pretend on nights like this, they already have the look of playboys who will still be here in ten years, doing the exact same thing. One of the guys, observing the girl I saw at the docks, knocks his friend's arm and says, loud enough that I can hear, "*Ja bi njoj dao metak*" (I'd like to shoot her a bullet).

The night envelops me as I walk down the street to the docks. A light wind breathing through the pine trees sends songs from a drinking party across the dark. I sit down on a stone bench and listen to the water clapping against the walls. Out at sea, a flickering light pinpoints a muttering engine on its way back. Whitish green halos of parting, rippling water float across the blackness. The engine slows and then stops and the boat whispers towards the dock.

No one seems to be at the helm of this ghostly vessel, maybe the one frozen on the horizon earlier, but then the lights flooding the dark sea are extinguished and others above the hold are turned on to reveal two men in rubber boots standing over a small mountain of still-wiggling and crawling fish and crabs. One of the men jumps onto the dock to secure the boat while the other pulls out some crates and starts sorting the catch. They work quickly and fearlessly, sticking their hands into the pile of pincers and throwing the inedible or too-small creatures over their shoulders into the water, where they land with quiet smacks. Sorted in no time, the pile reveals surprises right to the floor: slithery eels, strangely armoured shellfish, and a little turtle the guys examine and then toss back. They load the crates in a parked truck and drive into the night.

Alone again, I look across the bay, up at the stars. The rocks at my feet must have been gathered here by some kids, and I heave one out to hear the sound. Suddenly, the black water pulses gloriously with little lights as if the stars had fallen. For five minutes, they continue until finally the last persistent ones fade away. An appropriate sight on my last evening here, these plankton beautifully express the character of Povljana for me—a quiet place with humble secrets that flash at instants if I look closely enough. Tonight, Povljana will settle into memory and tomorrow, when I look again, I'll see a long, hot string of road where more secrets await.

8 ■ DALMATIA
Black Vulture, Old Wanderer

I'M UP AT SIX O'CLOCK TO CATCH THE BUS SOUTH to the ancient former capital of Dalmatia, Zadar. The peninsula across the bay is sharpening to sight and swallows have come out to hunt, replacing the bats. An empty village is eerier than a prairie wasteland. But I'm not alone. The old woman standing in the yard under a fig tree makes something cold run through me. She's watched me for two days now—watched others much longer than that, I imagine, before they put down asphalt or strung wires along the poles or even before they piled rocks for Sveti Nikola chapel. Her dark Indian face is alien to these parts, reminding me of the Vlach women who once wandered through this region.

What surprises me is her compulsion to go through the motions of being human, to pursue all the physical and emotional needs that flesh is heir to. Yesterday, for example, she showed up suddenly when I bought a litre of *travarica* from a local vendor—clear grape brandy flavoured by rosemary, thyme, and bay leaf. She stood so close I could smell her stale odour. Even though she didn't look directly at the bottle, she seemed to stare at it anyway. Her voice dragged like sheet metal over a road. "I was born in 1912. I was going to be a nun. I lived through three wars, but here I am today," she said, her hands stretched palms up as if she were excusing herself for still being around.

About to leave the yard for the bus stop the next morning, I pull out the Jack Daniel's bottle the biker gave me, still partly filled with *viljamovka*, and leave it on the wall. She'll wait until I'm gone awhile before snatching it up. Although illiterate, she might recognize the label's foreignness and assume the booze is foreign too. It might as well be. For her, Prigorje's pear orchards are as far away as Tennessee.

■

The bus is a brand-new swaying cruise liner with TV monitors that don't come on. It's an anomaly on the narrow, twisty stretch of concrete from Povljana to the main highway. Once we head east we pick up speed, racing through Pag's scrub-covered north, then across the bridge to the mainland. On the right, a tail of rock curls into the sea, baring up like some strange geological eruption, a crumbling toll house that's lost its crafted character and turned into a chunk of the island.

For a stretch, the landscape reverts to the flat bread-basket one around Zagreb, although the crops here are a month more mature. There are no other signs indicating how far south I am, but soon the road turns right, the earth becomes parched and blasted again, and the Adriatic shows up, sun-shimmered, rippled like a stretched-tight sheet held by two women drying and folding clothes on a hot blue day.

The people getting on for the short ride left to Zadar are mostly farmers on business or people going to market—old guys wearing tweed caps and white-and-blue shirts buttoned at their stubbled necks, stocky peasant women in white kerchiefs and aprons who carry covered wicker baskets, and high-school girls with fat black sunglasses perched on their heads and tight orange-and-white T-shirts wrapped across their breasts tightly like cellophane. In my khaki hat, T-shirt, and shorts, I'm so obviously a foreigner, an "American" tourist, that the passengers eye me curiously as they go down the aisle.

Soon the bus rolls into Zadar, along a tree-filled avenue lined by apartment rows and shops. Some sections closer to the centre are freshly painted in yellow and white, as buildings tend to be across the country, but these are pockmarked by bullet holes, as if someone meant to end this cleansing of the old Yugoslav landscape. The bus swings into the diesel chaos of the station. I have two hours before my bus south, enough time for a tour of the old town.

Zadar is built on a peninsula encircled by a wide concourse where boats and ferries destined for the rest of Croatia and Italy moor. By now more inured to the effects of old coastal towns, my first impressions are aesthetic. While Zadar has its undeniable attractions, it doesn't quite match Rab's integrated beauty. The sackings and bombings it suffered throughout history, most recently by the Allies in World War Two and the Serbs in the 1990s, have contributed to this effect.

I walk around somewhat aimlessly. By way of little Trg Vranjanima, I arrive by accident at the Franciscan Church and Monastery (founded apparently by Saint Francis on a journey to Syria in 1213, and the first Gothic one in Dalmatia). Liburnian gravestones, the ruins of Zadar's Roman Forum, and hints of the Roman town's former taverns and drainage system are still visible; a tall tower used as a pillory in the Middle Ages evokes a brutal time. I pause for a second in a fleeting connection with the people who ended up here, but images from stone are scant; they shiver briefly to life like holograms and then die. The place leaves me blind.

An impressive sight and the most culturally significant building for Croatian history is Sveti Donat church (ca. ninth to eleventh centuries). This massive pre-Romanesque drum-like structure and others of the same period are oddly designed, having irregular cross-shaped floors, slanted walls, uneven angles, and unsymmetrical cylinders of tambours.

> These buildings cannot be observed only as
> three-dimensional systems because ... [t]he annual
> movement of the sun ... determines the horizontal
> and vertical distribution of space ... Let us cite only
> one example: the slanted left wall at the main door
> of the St. Cross Church in Nin, which was also the
> first Croatian cathedral, was built in this fashion
> to ensure that the water in the font catch the last
> sunbeams on February 9, the day of St. Ambrosius

deacon, who was the patron saint of the Benedictines in Nin ... The church's interior and exterior were designed to measure time, especially the spring and autumn equinoxes and the winter and summer solstices. The Church of St. Cross is a clock, a calendar, and a temple all in one.[1]

Along with Sveti Križ (St. Cross), the former seat of Bishop Grgur Ninski (who promoted the Slavonic liturgy at the Council of Salona in 1059), and various structures throughout Croatia, Sveti Donat is the remaining evidence of the ancient Kingdom of Croatia.

The Church of Sveti Šimun (St. Simeon) has its own claim to historical significance and is admired more for the sarcophagus it contains than for its architecture. Resting on two marble and two bronze angels cast from guns wrested by the Venetians from the Turks in the seventeenth century, the box contains the mummified body of St. Simeon the Just, who allegedly took baby Jesus in his arms and proclaimed him Messiah on the eighth day, the day of Jesus' circumcision.

About his arrival in Zadar, there is this story. A ship crippled by the Bura limped to dock in 1213 or 1273 and spilled from its cargo a knight or nobleman who stumbled wearily into the sanctuary of a monastery. At the outset of his journey to the Holy Land, his mission evidently consumed him and gave him strength, but arriving in Zadar—where men who wandered the dark interior of the Balkans swept through, bringing with them ideas of unbelievers—an illness of some kind wasted him and he died. On his deathbed, his whispered revelation hissed dully in the stone chamber, stunning the credulous monks. They immediately hoisted the cedar chest in which Simeon rested and displayed it in a church, where it began performing miracle cures that spread its fame up and down Dalmatia. Elizabeth, daughter of *ban* Stjepan Kotromanić II of Bosnia and wife of King Ludovik (Louis d'Anjou) of Hungary, who delivered Zadar from Venetian siege, came to the city in 1371, furtively cracked off one of the Saint's fingers and stuck it in her bosom. Versions of the story go that the finger filled with maggots, or that Simeon struck her stone blind or caused her chest to seize. After returning the relic to the body, where it miraculously reattached itself, her health was restored except for a shrivelled hand she bore to the end of her days. In contrition, she had Francesco di Antonio da Sesto of Milan commissioned to oversee the carving of silver-gilt bas-reliefs so intricate and beautiful that they outdid the rest of the church. Every October 8, St. Simeon's reliquary is opened and his mummified head glares out a warning to all unbelievers.

■

Zadar shares with other coastal towns a similarly strife-ridden, arduous past that is evident in its panoply of architectural styles. The Liburnian tribe of Illyrians who founded it, Romans, Byzantines, Franks, Venetians, Hungarians, Austrians, French, Italians, and Serbs all controlled or had influence over Zadar. For a while around the eleventh and twelfth centuries, it was the most prized, populous city in Dalmatia and the object of a see-sawing struggle between Venice and the Kingdom of Croatia and then the dual kingdom of Hungarian-Croatia. But it was as the administrative centre of Venetian Dalmatia that Zadar acquired its dominant architectural mode or feeling, and so, like Rab, it forever projected an aura of that age with its urbane houses, churches, and little architectural virtues, which somehow survived invasions and bombardments. Yet that aura has also survived the architectural suturing of style with style and epoch with epoch, as Zadar gradually was stitched into a different city altogether, probably unrecognizable to the citizens who knew it so long ago. This is hardly worth mentioning about Dalmatia, although it strikes me as especially pronounced in Zadar, and probably more so in Dubrovnik.

Building styles are not the only measure of a city's evolution. In *The Near East* (1913), his memoir of travels through Dalmatia, Greece, and Constantinople, Robert Hichens experienced a world now lost forever, not only because the people he described dressed and, therefore, seemed to *be* so different, but because Zadar looked Balkan in a way that northern Croatia never did:

> There is a wildness of the near East in this medieval
> Italian town. Against the somber greys and browns of
> façades, set in the deep shadows of the paved alleys
> which are Zara's streets, move brilliant colors, scarlet

and silver, blue and crimson and silver. Multitudes of
coins and curious heavy ornaments glitter on the
caps and dresses of women. Enormous boys and
great, striding men, brave in embroidered jackets,
with bright-red caps too small for the head, silver
buttons, red sashes stuck full of weapons and other
impedimenta, gaiters, and pointed shoes, march
hither and thither, calmly intent on some business
which has brought them in from the outlying districts.[2]

Although these men were probably Dalmatians, they projected a
look of a region long cross-fertilized culturally. Also, Hichens saw
Zadar's public, business, or formal side, which was still related to its
folk identity. That connection doesn't exist any longer. If men here
wear business suits, the suits aren't related to anything regionally cultural about the men. I have to look closer to see through their international sameness, beyond their casual corporate clothing, to imagine
whether they could replace Hichens' men of long ago. No doubt some
of these living versions—tall, dark brown or black-haired, with growling
voices and strong hands gesturing, snaking out cigarette smoke—
could turn into those parading by Hichens. It takes more time to undo
deeply embedded cultural traits, yet these too will be subject to change
eventually, however hereditary they may seem.

I end up sitting on a bench across from a café that's still Yugo-
spare, attended on by rude, underpaid help. A sour-looking waiter
gazes in the direction of his only customer—an old man buried in a
newspaper. The man tosses back the rest of his brandy or maraschino
liqueur (a local specialty), and the glass flashes like a chunk of
sunlight in his hand. Getting up to leave, he accidentally bumps the
glass off the table and it breaks on the tiled floor. The waiter strides
across the terrace. After a short argument, the old man stuffs some
bills into the waiter's shirt pocket and walks in my direction, volleying
a loud "*kurac!*" behind him, a more vulgar version of "prick."

He sits down. His veined face is flushed under his tweed cap.
"Sonofabitch," he says. "Always been like this here." A fat hand
sweeps around the square. His white shirt is unbuttoned to the middle
of his chest, his belly hanging over his belt. "These *tovari* (donkeys)

never knew how to treat guests," he says, using the pejorative slang for the lazy Dalmatian. "Same as before, just more expensive." His round jowls are nicked from shaving and look clown-like, but his eyes are soberingly intelligent, putting me on guard for irony.

"This country will forever be fucked," he goes on with no irony at all. "But if the Germans took over, see...," he says, a hand gesture finishing his thoughts. Like people I'd met in northern Croatia, he has an inviolable faith in German know-how and productivity. Let them take over the coast and see what they do with it.

"I'm from Krajina, man. They burned us out of our houses. I go from place to place. Soon gotta sell one of these," he says, his thumb pressing on a golden molar. Rather than return after Croatia's Oluja offensive into the Serb enclave of Krajina, he went in the opposite direction, further into Croatia, where he's been moving around ever since. He's a bricklayer by trade who used to go on *teren* (contracts away from home) and now stays with fellow labourers from his construction days. Like the old woman in Povljana, he lives on the margins of his new world. But unlike her, he's a newer kind of outsider because he's a self-imposed Croat refugee produced by a war the Croats themselves won. Born in the borderland of Krajina, he now finds himself a wandering hired hand. Behind his tough exterior. I detect a certain desperation that probably haunts his private self. What does the future hold for a man like this? How long can he go on? While he has the option of going back to Krajina, there may not be much of a home to return to.

I say goodbye and walk towards the bus station. I arrive just as the drivers fling the last pieces of luggage into the storage bin. Forebodingly, the air vents above my head are unresponsive and the windows are built shut. "You still have time to get out," I think. Almost immediately the drivers hop up and shut the door. My fate is sealed; we're on our way.

The jagged mountains that crash straight into the Adriatic have taken the highway and twisted it into tortured shapes. The bus turns sharply, sometimes descending to sea level and then climbing hundreds of yards higher. Concrete blocks, menhirs, and steel guard-rails, which are ominously bent or missing sections, are a last defence against a fall off the steep cliffs. There are more intimidating roads in Croatia, like the one from Zadar inland across the Velebits, but few are more spectacular. John Berger has described this sort of landscape as "romantic," always "at the edge, at the end, of the possible."[3]

I get a picture of former times in Dalmatia from coves with their dories and stone houses. Now hotels, private *pansions*, and restaurants are ubiquitous as well. New settlements that sprang up after the construction of the Magistrala highway in the 1960s straddle the road or line the seashore to capitalize on tourism. That said, there are still beautiful old towns with long histories along the way to Split, like Primošten and Trogir—two former islands just off the coast, now joined to the mainland by a causeway and a bridge.

Trogir is the more notable architecturally, listed as a UNESCO World Heritage Site for its medieval centre. For example, the west portal of Sveti Lovrijenac (St. Lawrence) cathedral (1240) is a true master-work. A profusion of religious iconography, scenes from legends, and archetypal moments are run together with virtuoso-like skill. The peasant trimming grapevines represents the arrival of spring; the old man butchering a wild boar symbolizes cold December. The work was carved by a local master, Radovan, whose name is inscribed in the stone, along with his proud declaration, "Most excellent in his art."

Trogir was also the site of a notable military confrontation. In 1242, Bela IV of Hungary was besieged here by Mongols after having raced from one Croat fortification to another ahead of their conquests. Too numerous, too savage, too mobile—since they were mounted and journeyed lightly, fuelling themselves partly off the blood of their beasts—the Mongols had the town at their mercy. But Trogir's defenders refused to hand the king over, probably suspecting they would be attacked anyway. The city's destruction seemed at hand as the Mongols waited for their orders on the mainland outside the town walls. Just when the invaders were ready to sack the town with all the force they could muster, a dusty rider brought news of the death of their Khan, Ogadai, and reportedly because of an uncertain succession, they turned their horses towards the Balkan hinterland and never came back.

On the day I visit, more prosaic things are happening. Workers in an alley have lifted a sewer grate and are prodding sludge with iron rods. Tourists wander through the main square. An eighty-year-old drunk loiters in a café at the town's entrance; he offers me his moist hand and then falls asleep in his chair still holding on, still hoping for a free drink.

■

I travel south. I'm feeling the distance from my anchoring point in the north, less in the body than in the psyche. This dislocation could be caused by Dalmatia's arid landscape, a landscape that's wearing me down with its austerity. Once I return I'll be grateful for the lush hills and flatlands of Prigorje as if they were somehow the reason for my well-being, or at least were integrated within my intuited sense of home. And then there's the distance I feel because of language: I miss speaking and hearing English. I want to swim in it like a fish in water, fluent again. But both here and in rural Prigorje there's not much chance of that.

That night I sleep in a cavernous house owned by an old widow whom I come across as if in answer to these questions of home and distance. This has always been her place. Like other old widows on the coast, she's dressed in black from top to bottom. Her youthful energy and her place astound me. The earth in her garden, though stony and apparently inhospitable, sustains row upon row of bay leaf, thyme, basil, paprika, tomatoes, green peppers, lettuce, onions, leeks, beans, and peas. Her storage room is stacked six feet high with plastic crates of potatoes, arranged by size, most of which she'll have to give or throw away. About ten barrels of homemade wine and a juniper-based liqueur called *pelinkovac* ring a cold room. Groves of juniper, pecan, almond, olive, and fig stretch hundreds of metres behind the house, eventually becoming the countryside.

The land is covered by sedge grass, rocks, and maquis. A tough land. But as others have over the centuries before her, the widow has drawn the most out of it, made it answer to her labour. There's little that is unique about this relationship to the earth in the history of the world, but as always when I meet someone like her, I'm reminded of the work and intricate knowledge that made such a life possible. Although she would consider Canada a distant, alien place, her mentality seems much like those who settled great swaths of it. She shares with them a conviction about what the earth can provide. And although it's easy for a suburbanite like myself to romanticize, to have the luxury of envy, I feel that she is comfortable with her destiny, comfortable in her skin.

I hit the road again. The first Sunday of every August has been marked in Sinj, north of Split, by the Sinjska *Alka* tilting tournament, a commemoration of a victory over the Turks in 1715 in a battle for the town's fortress. Grandstands crammed with spectators line the corridor, where knights on horseback, in brown drum-like hats and black jackets brocaded with gold, thunder towards suspended rings to pierce them with their lances. Points are awarded for hitting the bull's eye and the outer sections of the alka, two concentric rings linked by three bars. The beating of hooves, dust rising and settling, the swelling of voices, the pageantry of colour, and the smell of roasting lamb all add to the festival atmosphere. At moments, the present fades, and the past, with all its masculine heroism, its assertion of freedom from the Turks, comes to life around me.

9 ◨ DALMATIAN ISLANDS
Hvar, Brač, Korčula

WIND RATTLES THE WOODEN SHUTTERS AND PALE sunlight through the slats reveals grey whitewashed walls, a brass crucifix, and a big armorite closet hovering on my right. There's nothing fancy about this room in a local family's house, but for nine dollars a night, I'll take it.

It's just after seven o'clock on Sunday morning. The shutters won't let me sleep anymore, so I throw them open and view the roofs of Stari Grad. The island of Hvar's "old town" is a dense mass of stone a kilometre away, founded in 385 BC as a Greek colony called Pharos. The crumbled remains of Greek fortifications are still evident, but the place has the simple feel of a Slavic settlement, like so many Dalmatian towns.

I think of my brief stay the night before in the industrial port city of Split, from where I sailed to Hvar. While Split is still visited for its own old town, and especially the world's largest existing Roman palace, completed by Diocletian in 305 AD, the modern city is a sprawling riot of grey concrete Lego blocks and noise.

As I step out into the morning, the only noise I hear is the ringing of bells, shredded by wind. Otherwise, Stari Grad is silent. The storm is still driving through and the heat has stayed off so far. The town is built on one side and at the end of a narrow fjord bordered by steep pine-covered hills, nearly mountains. Cobbled streets lead me in no particular direction, closing around me as an old town always does around a stranger. Even though I end up in its dusty heart I feel more locked out than ever. Shutters are sealed tight. Bells keep ringing parishioners I haven't seen to the church I haven't found, although every corner brings the sounds closer. A broken stone crucifix that's missing its right arm stares out of a hollow dugout in a house's wall, the window cracked and unlocked. Gutted bee carcasses and pine needles from last year are strewn along the walls.

Eventually, I follow a lane that leads to a little square and a church. A stooped woman wearing the usual black garb inches in shuffling steps towards the open door. A priest swoops past in his billowing robes and disappears into the church's black interior. The bells vibrate terrifically into the sky in one final peal.

Inside, a clutch of old women in the pews waits for the mass to begin. The only light is from a few guttering candles and little holes in the walls that serve as windows. Swallows fly in and out through the open door. The service begins with the priest intoning solemnly, his voice echoing dully, sounding as if it were arriving from somewhere long ago, or were his compatriots' collective voice across a thousand years, not the living one in his warm throat. The voice is hypnotic and the heads in front of me nod and bodies lean against each other. The women will soon drift away! I feel a bit stupefied too.

I walk in the direction that I picture the sea to be in. Wind whistles through my ears and clears up my head. On one side of the inlet where the town lies, a shaded promenade curls along the sea through the forests. Away from town on the other side, in the sun, are white concrete piers and patios with inlaid stone, belonging to a waterfront hotel. The hotel is a massive, white, inelegant structure, as communist ones tend to be. It's also completely empty. Not a soul disturbs me, although it's perversely possible that a waiter might suddenly pop out of the trees and tell me to move on or pay up.

Today the water is clear and cold. I front-crawl ferociously back and forth to warm up, and then get out when the cold somewhere at the core of me starts to take hold. The wind has had its effect. I dry off, warm up, let my eyes wander over the mountains and the body of water in front of me, and then slip into a reverie in which images arrive and merge and leave like lap dissolves.

... Tourists are coming, carrying towels and air mattresses and beach balls, the women with backcombed bees'-nest hair and the men in flared Fortrel pants and sideburns. Waiters are carrying straw brooms to sweep away last fall's pine cones and needles, and toting plastic umbrellas that slide into concrete supports. Someone turns on a transistor radio, and a scratchy version of "Marijana" ("Sweet little Marijana, I'll wait for you until the dawn"), followed by something by the Carpenters, floats across the bay. Then the place is empty again and stray bits of paper are whisked away by the wind. A commotion begins somewhere near the hotel. A dignified older couple arrives and sits stiffly at a canopied table beside an extravagant buffet served by waiters and watched over by sombre men in suits and dark glasses. The woman is wearing a matronly pink dress and matching pink hat on the crown of her head (it looks like a fez but is categorically not), and the man wears his hair slicked back, thick gold glasses, and a military khaki suit embroidered on his chest with bars of colour. A crowd assembled across the inlet by the town is waving large flags with red stars and shouting something, the words muffled at first and chaotic, merging with the music from the hotel, two syllables rising into the air, assembling, honed into clarity: TI-TO, TI-TO, TI-TO...

There's nothing grandiose or heroic about the young guide who meets me in the foyer of Petar Hektorović's crumbling fortified mansion, Tvrdalj. Tomislav Alaupović is surprised to see me and pleased I've come. Nut-brown hair sweeps boyishly off his forehead and blue eyes assess me peacefully from his tanned, handsome face, regarding me with a trust and understanding people rarely possess, as if he intuitively understands all my good qualities and would gladly let me show them. "I take you inside, yes?" he asks, showing me through to the arcaded terrace and a large pool filled with dark jade water.

The surface is thickly still, unhealthily solid, and a black mass appears to shiver slightly near the bottom. A few parts break off and waver to the surface. Fish! The pool is filled with dark mullets, hovering together in the morning and then circling and rising to the surface when food is dropped, silver-scaled when light strikes them. We watch in silence for a while, my guide appreciative, as if seeing them for the first time.

"The salt and spring water has not change many month," he informs me. "It is not good for fish, the different chemicals and temperatures, and taking fish out is problem also." The ancients were said to keep red mullets in basins of sea water by their tables so they could savour the spectacle of colour and dance before choosing their dinner.

My guide shows me around. Tvrdalj was begun by Hektorović in 1514 as a stronghold against Turkish attack, although it was never finished in his lifetime. Various inscriptions in Latin are carved in stone around the place. The original wells are still here. Some things have been introduced to portray traditional Hvar life: a copper vessel for washing with ashes, a sort of sledge for hot coals to warm a bed, an old wine press in the cellar, and a canon used since 1885 to break up hail clouds. The guide leads me to the sun-dappled garden courtyard of mint plants, fig and olive trees, and exotic Mediterranean flora. Hektorović himself (1487–1572) tended a garden here, and it serves as a wonderful example of his creative energies, and a counterpart to his long poem *Ribanje i Ribarsko Prigovaranje* (*Fishing and Fishermen's Conversations*).

Widely called the first realist poem in Croatian literature, it comes across now as an "imposed idealization."[1] Its English translator argues that the poem's realism derives from its generally objective, non-figurative language, its psychological profile of two fishermen who accompany him on his trip to Brač and Šolta, and some simple experiences like fishing and drinking wine. Written as an epistle to a relative, the poem also contains introspective lyrics, and elegiac and dramatic elements in which the fishermen are given voice, including stiff Christian moralizing. Critics with a penchant for anachronism point out the democratic nature of the work, since Hektorović, a nobleman, sailed with two commoners. It's true, though, that his genuine embrace of his companions situates the work within a humanist tradition, and thus to a certain extent outside the literary and social conventions of the time.

Alaupović seems proud of Hektorović's cultural importance, and proud of the peaceful and salutary place itself. His enthusiasm might be more than just role-playing; it could be born from wider nationalistic feelings that made him volunteer for war duty. To fight for Croatia also meant to preserve its culture. But when asked about his war experience, he goes quiet, saying only, "When someone shoots, you shoot too."

We return to the foyer, where he hands me a postcard of the fish pool, the arcades, and a red stamp of Hektorović's emblem: three diagonal stripes above a bull. We shake hands. In the last image I have of him, he's standing at the foot of the tower, waving. And so I'm glad because he can never be a disappointment to me, outside of Tvrdalj and the poet he is bound to forever in my mind.

Built during Napoleonic rule, the road from Stari Grad to the main city of Hvar is a sheer climb of ferocious switchbacks cresting the mountainous island and descending sharply on the other side. From so high up, Stari Grad is a toy town and the fjord a narrow blue finger trimmed by an enamel of white coasts.

The driver has left the doors and emergency hatches open, but the air blowing through is not as stifling as it was during the last few days. A powerful man with telephone-pole arms, the driver takes disconcertingly casual glances over his shoulder to chat with the only other passenger, another driver. With every turn he seems about to tip the bus over the precipices, but veers it back adeptly. Soon I become used to the rhythm, realizing he could probably negotiate this road from memory.

When we enter the interior, houses appear like forlorn orphans— shutters closed, roofs sinking, and people long gone. Some living settlements and small stores show up too, but not a single person. Below the road in the valleys, amid pine trees and holm oak and rock piles and walls that look like monuments to some alien presence, are little gardens and vineyards and lavender fields, shimmering light purple. The farmers who cultivate these oases seemed to have dropped from the sky to do their work, then disappeared again in the wood's seclusion.

A view of Hvar from the stairs leading to the Kaštel, 1996.

On the long descent to the city, we finally sight another human: a scrawny, bare-chested, middle-aged guy, nougat brown, steering a column of sheep along the road with a shirt on his head to protect him from the sun. I glimpse his spectrally gaunt face and the blackness where his teeth should be. The afterthought of a beard stubbles his thin jaw and scruffy black hair sticks out past his ears. Rabid eyes look fiercely out of his face.

He's left behind in a flash, and then Hvar appears below as if in answer—a sudden awakening to culture and tourism. Built on a hill beside the sea, Hvar is a city of stairs overlooking the open sea and an archipelago of eleven, small forested islands ringed with white stones, known as the Pakleni Otoci (hell's islands). The houses hunker down against the heat; piled on top of each other they seem to cascade to the rectangular harbour in a rush to cool off. A promenade unfurls along the coves in the hazy distance. That's where I'll go.

Just after noon, the sun is nearing its searing apex, and no one is fool enough to be outside except me. The promenade takes me past more communist-era hotel complexes and pebbled coves, some with stairs of concrete poured over rock. Squat palms, pines, and juniper bushes crowd the edge of the path. I find an empty white pebbled beach about two kilometres from Hvar and dive into the water; it's far warmer than Stari Grad's and light green, like a transparent jade foil rippled by steady breezes. A concrete pier fifty metres from the beach narrows the tiny bay's opening, and then there's open sea—sun-glittered and darkening eventually, still green in my range for today.

The bells of Sveti Stjepan are announcing another mass. Unlike the ghostly pealing this morning, these bells evoke only a cultural rich-ness, which was missing in Stari Grad. Indeed, Hvar replaced Stari Grad as the island's capital in the thirteenth century, and wherever one looks there are signs of Hvar's image as a refined, cultured resort. Palm trees, like mute exotic guards, line the harbour, just as they do in the south of France. The upper storey of the Arsenal is one of the oldest theatres still standing in Europe (1612), and nearby is the largest square in Dalmatia. High atop the north hill, accessible by a winding-staired walkway, is the thirteenth-century Kaštel, where many citizens retreated during the 1571 raid of the corsair Uluz-Ali.

People off the ferry are still milling around by the water, and old women are watching eagerly for new visitors in need of lodgings. The stairs up into the southern part of Hvar are spaced out by stretches of slick flagstones and concrete inclines. Small courtyards tidily adorned with vines, white roses, and other flowers are quiet shaded spots for meals or naps. In one street, a man with a white shock of hair, wearing a white undershirt and blue shorts, sits on a pail and repairs a fishnet that drapes off a balcony overhead like fantastic hair in a fairy tale. The net is enormous and it billows around his knees. An hour later, he's still at it, deftly sewing frayed strands and showing no signs of being tired. Like Štefek's distillation of *šljivovica*, this man's work has become a way to pass time, a diversion, though it does have a practical purpose. The lives of these two men are obviously different, yet their intimacy with the smallest actions and the care inherent in their physical labour is something they share, something for which young Croats I know have much less patience.

I get a ride back to Stari Grad with one of these young Croats who has come to Hvar on a "private job" about which he's rather vague. A tough, charming, good-looking Dalmatian with blond hair, military short, and intense green eyes, Igor wants to make a buck the quick way.

"*Pijem pivo, jebi me se živo*" (I drink beer, I fuck everything), he calls out to some guys outside the café in Stari Grad where he's invited me for a drink. "We all went to war together," he says, smoke from his cigarette enclosing us too intimately for my liking. "*Drugi su pičkin dim*" (the others are cunt smoke [that is, worthless]).

He continues, "I don't have time for the diaspora who didn't fight. I wouldn't talk to them." For a second, I think he's making an unsubtle reference to me, but I realize I'm not a true Croat in his mind.

"I tell you, when I got my uniform...," he says, stopping and turning away. The sun on his brown and usually emotionless face reveals a spasm of feeling. I remember the soldier on Rab, and then my guide this morning and the different form taken by his nationalism. A picture of life for the compatriots of Stari Grad emerges—camaraderie that outsiders can never be part of, late nights and drinking and women for fun. Such aimlessness might be written off as the release after war. This young man is in it for the long haul. "Marriage is stale, man," he laughs.

After saying goodbye, I walk around town one last time. It has become a habit of mine to store away sights of a place I may never visit again. My voyage down the coast in 1996 is nearly over. I have a strong sense that the circumstances that made the trip so unique—the tourist-free regions resulting from war paranoia, the lingering effects of battle in the psyches of people, the surge of nationalist euphoria in a newly independent country, and my intense experience on the road to Pag—may never occur again in my lifetime. The feeling I'm left with is that of having been the only visitor to the museum, of having witnessed a fleeting period in Croatia's history.

I return to southern Dalmatia in August 1997. The island of Brač rises in a blue-green dawn as my plane tilts towards Bol airport. Reaching the resort a few hours later, I notice more tourists than the year before and it takes me awhile to adjust to sharing the sort of place I had virtually to myself. I seclude myself well away from the packed peninsular Zlatni Rat beach—a beach that made Brač one of Croatia's top destinations, but overrated compared to the coves around the island. The emerald water here is so pristine—it's second to none in the world.

Others are enjoying it too. A couple in the cove next to mine is making love in the shallows, the woman rising and falling rhythmically to the swells pushing onto the shore, holding him by the shoulders, his hands on her hips, their brown skin shining against the sea.

I close my eyes against the fierce sun. Lying on this pebbled shore, I hear water lapping near my feet, crickets in the swaying whispering pine forest behind, and farther away, at the edge of my hearing, the shouts of children playing. Early in the day, and in certain months, you can still experience this Brač. But not perhaps to the absolute sensual perfection of this moment. The war, which had emptied the coast of visitors, now seems securely in the past.

Beyond these coves and the tourist traps along the sea is a different Brač altogether. The interior is dry terrain like much of the Mediterranean; there are junipers, olive trees, and gaunt terraced vineyards clinging to the stony ground; the aroma of sage, rosemary, and other herbs I can't identify; paved roads and rocky trails traversing the island much like those on Rab; and if you're smack-dab in the middle of Brač, flattish as it is in places, the feeling of being very close to the sky. At one time, Brač was almost entirely covered in vineyards, such that most of the population was involved at some point in pruning, spraying, harvesting, mashing, and shipping the final product off the land. In the late nineteenth century, Brač (and indeed Dalmatia) was a major exporter of wine to France, which had been ravaged by the phylloxera (vine lice) epidemic. After phylloxera spread to Dalmatia, decimating vines, the industry never fully rebounded.

The real story about Brač, though, may be the white limestone at its core. The island's quarries (the oldest opening around 300 BC) provided stone for Diocletian's Palace in Split, the Cathedral in Trogir, and other buildings and monuments throughout Dalmatia and around the world, including Canada's World War One Vimy Ridge Memorial in Flanders—but not the White House in Washington, according to its own historical association. The old quarrying days, when men worked with tools forged in the quarry's blacksmith shop and horses pulled huge slabs to the north shore, where they were loaded on boats and shipped around the world, are long gone. Gone too are the spacious cutting shops where upwards of fifty masons used to cut and chisel stone by hand.

Other kinds of traditional life have either disappeared or been greatly scaled back. An emigrant from Brač who settled in British Columbia described the old world of shepherding to me: the two-hundred-year-old sardine cannery in his home village of Postira, the export of sweet morello cherries to chocolate factories in Germany and Switzerland, and the commercial wine and olive oil business of his father.

Like other places in Dalmatia, Brač has been depopulated, partly during the late nineteenth century when the wooden shipbuilding industry couldn't adjust to the steamship. Many Dalmatians immigrated to South America, where they thought their old ways could be sustained anew. They arrived at the bottom of the world and saw similar stark, wind-carved islands (albeit less similar than they appeared on maps). Thirty thousand Croats now live in the earth's southernmost city, Punta Arenas, capital of Chile's Magallenes province in Tierra del Fuego.

Croats have been great travellers, maybe none greater than Marco Polo (ca. 1254–1324). The descent to his alleged birthplace in Korčula is guarded by cypresses that pierce the sky like minarets. Bats are fluttering in the squares on the evening that I arrive. Like so many other towns on Croatia's Adriatic, Korčula is a beautiful outcropping of stone, shaped like a fish with streets like bones growing off its spine. Called Korkyra Melaina by the first Greek settlers, then Corcyra Nigra by the Romans for its dark pine woods, Korčula became "the choice seat of Venetian power in these waters, her strong arsenal, the place for the building of her galleys."[2]

The next day, I go to Marco Polo's house. Swallows are screeching and swooping around the cathedral. The house is a ruin located on a side street with steep stairs, a plaque, and a ticket collector. The place could pass as the sort of outback origins of a man who goes on to much bigger things. When I ask the ticket collector about Marco Polo, he mumbles something about the documents that prove everything.

"Which documents?" I ask.

"The documents. Family records and so on."

"How come the Venetians say he was born there?"

"How should I know? Go ask the travel agency. Look, do you want to go in or what?" He puts his glasses back on and starts reading the paper again.

Korčulans say the Depolo family lived here for centuries, that Mate Polo (uncle of Marco) applied to the town's administration for rights to purchase land for a shipyard in 1230, that Marco Polo was captured by the Genoese near Korčula during a battle with the Venetians in 1298 (subsequently dictating his famous travels), and that the house in question was given to the Depolo family in 1400, seventy-six years after Marco's death.

While locals may be right, the rewriting of history in this part of the world and its integration in the national consciousness and school curricula also suggest a need to put the area on the map. Common under communist regimes (the erased Trotsky image), such rewriting is now practised by Croat patriots at all levels, especially those operating the tourist machine. For example, besides assertions about the White House, which were propagated in the Yugo days, some tourist guides claim that Eduard (Slavoljub) Penkala invented the first pen (sometimes fountain, sometimes ballpoint), thereby giving it his name to this day, although the truth appears to be that he patented a mechanical *pencil* in 1906—and that while he lived for a time in Zagreb, he wasn't a Croat at all, born in Slovakia to a Polish father and Dutch mother. Other sources say Faust Vrančić, author of a book on mechanics and inventions, *Machinae Novae* (1615), designed, constructed, and tested the first parachute in history, and even that his first sketch is mistakenly attributed to Leonardo da Vinci. More widely acknowledged outside of Croatia is that soldiers of the Croat cavalry in Louis XIV's army, the Royale-Cravate, introduced the world to the necktie.

■

The seven men on a bench near the marina are such old friends that they don't look at each other when they talk. They're chatting or watching people go by or staring into space. When I start a conversation, the first one who talks answers with another question: "Where are you from?" Like most of the others, he's wearing a white shirt with an undershirt visible underneath, suspenders, pants, and sandals. In his knuckled hand is a cane that he swats around to emphasize his points.

"I'm from Canada."

"Where was your father born?"

"Near Samobor."

"Ah yeah, Samobor. That's OK then." They're trying to determine what kind of outsider I am, as if they have different categories and different ways of dealing with them. I'm not on the highest rung (a local or Dalmatinac), but not on the lowest either (a complete foreigner or enemy). "We got all types comin' here," another says.

"Right, all types," two others add, like a chorus. "They come and then they go." They gaze out at the marina, looking neither at each other nor at me.

"What should the world know about Korčula?" I ask, in an effort to get them talking.

"Tell the world we got our freedom," answers the guy with the cane. "We got something they're not gonna take away again."

"He said it," another adds. "We got no one to answer to."

They go silent awhile, and I take the cue to go.

The following afternoon, I drive into the country, where I come across the most beautiful beach I've seen in Croatia. The way from Korčula leads inland at first and then strikes towards the sea on the southern side of the island. I'm high up and overlooking the open Adriatic, where the road clings precariously to the flanks of the coast. From here, the air and the colours seem purified of every contaminant by some radiant acid. On a concrete guardrail, a black graffito reads "Death to Serbs."

The crumbling blacktop becomes indecisive at points—either fallen away completely or full of potholes big enough to eat my car. No signs tell me where to go, even though Pupnatska Luka is mentioned in tourist brochures. Eventually, I see the half-moon beach, turquoise water, and a "road" leading down, so viciously rocky that it makes the car shake like an epileptic.

Captain Mile advertises himself with a sign on his house. He's standing on the white pebble beach, folding nets lethargically; he's wearing a floppy leather hat pierced by a feather, and his breasts hang over his Santa Claus belly. When I ask him if the boat in the bay is his, he looks at me and says, "What the hell is that to you?"

"Just starting a conversation," I say.

"Who the hell are you to come here and ask a question like that? In front of a man's own house."

"Sorry."

"Why don't you go back where you came from."

"I can be here if I want," I retort, starting to get angry. "This isn't your beach."

"You need to learn how to behave."

"People were friendly everywhere in Croatia. I got offered wine, meals in Prigorje, everything. They were never rude."

"I'll tell you why they're like that. It's because they don't have the sea."

What can I do except laugh? To show him he doesn't own the Adriatic, I get into my trunks and take a swim. This encounter reminds me of a story that made news across Croatia in 1999. A Jadrolinija ferry worker in Split refused to allow a woman and her two kids on the ferry for Supetar because her car bore the emblem of Dinamo Zagreb (a soccer club). He told her to take it off or miss the boat. She relented because of her children, but soon afterward her husband related the story to the media. The ferry worker may have been venting enmity for a rival team in the north, even redressing years of living on the fringes of political power, and investing his own club, Hajduk Split, with importance in the waning of real cultural identity. The rivalry between Zagreb and Split is sometimes antagonistic and goes beyond mere soccer hooliganism. At the time when this book was published, the rivalry's political aspect was evident too, because Split had emerged as a centre for rightist opposition to the post-Tudjman, pro-western government in Zagreb.

It would be pernicious to excoriate Dalmatians en masse because of such incidents. But after my experience at the beach I leave with an unfortunate tendency to endow even innocuous encounters with people, as well as cultural ceremonies intended mainly for tourists, with social and political connotations. For example, I think it's possible to see Korčula's Moreška Sword Dance as a ceremonial expression of Dalmatia's attitudes towards outsiders. The dramatic dance, transplanted from Spain to the Adriatic via Spanish sailors, and possibly to Korčula from Sicily during Venetian rule, re-enacts a battle between Christ and Moors (or Arabs and Moors, since it remains unclear whether the dance was originally a Spanish or Moorish one). A Black King and a White King are fighting for the latter's Muslim fiancée, who has been abducted by the Black King and appears in the Korčula version to have converted to Christianity. Her love for the White King justifies the battle in universal terms of justice and honour, though it is undergirded by religious and cultural disdain for the "infidel." Two armies of dancers, dressed to the nines in caps, coin-spangled vests, white breeches, and boots clash to music provided by a band. Needless to say, the White King triumphs and is reunited with his betrothed.

No Korčulan connects intimately to this story or consciously applies it in everyday relations with outsiders, but it seems like an objective correlative for a general defiance. Viewed favourably, it speaks of a toughness, independence, and haughtiness that grew over centuries in the tumult and cross-currents of cultures in the Adriatic.

10 ■ DUBROVNIK
The Mad Muse

My trip down the coast ends before the highway finishes its last turns in Croatia, abutting on Montenegro. I've come to the walled city of Dubrovnik, still nominally the pearl of the Adriatic. Dubrovnik is an architectural wonder, but what Byron said in the nineteenth century about the only comparable Adriatic city, Venice, is also true about Dubrovnik at the end of the twentieth: it's a jewel whose shine has come off with time, a city suffering from entropy.

That said, the comparison in my mind between the reputed Dubrovnik and the real one can't spoil the city for me (an experience Walker Percy called the "loss of the creature"). Dubrovnik retains its allure from the second I step inside its walls, if not the sublime beauty its admirers describe.

After the winding trip from Split, I stumble out of the stifling bus at the western opening to the town, the Pile gate, where the new and old world meet. The station is a congested circular looping past cafés, travel agencies, and a shiny architecture of motorbikes. Over a wooden drawbridge that crosses a moat strewn with fallen oranges, I pass Dubrovnik's patron saint, St. Blaise, who cradles a model of the city as it was before the catastrophic earthquake of 1667. Stairs descend to an elegant, spacious promenade, the limestone Stradun, which stretches to the eastern side of the city, its glistening flagstones repaired by stonemasons after the destruction wreaked by Montenegrin and Serb forces in 1991.

Just the ample dimensions and allotment of the Stradun's space, the line of buildings guiding the eye to the end of the street, which concludes at the majestic bell tower, give the place an immediate aura of culture, urbanity, and design not quite duplicated anywhere on the coast. Because the street is wide, it feels like a square—but because it's long and channels the movements of people in one direction or another, it's cinematic rather than painterly; that is, it encourages people to experience it as a fluid event—to travel, not cluster in fixed groups. How suitable this is, since Dubrovnik was a place of trade for centuries, where goods were packed off by caravans or unloaded from tall ships, where the Mediterranean, the Balkan hinterland, and the east flowed through.

Today, Dubrovnik seems alienated from traditional life. No old women sit on stools outside their doors sewing lace, and no old men drag fishing lines along a dock or dream the colours of their dories or perform some action known to be characteristic of the place itself. Dubrovnik has never been Pag. It was the opposite of provincial for centuries. Yet peasants who lived in outlying villages and fishermen and sailors who really made the city function could always be seen in the streets, commingling on the Stradun. They were visibly part of the city's life.

In the 1930s, Rebecca West ascribed to peasants she saw on the Corso (as she Italianized Stradun) the need "to escape from the horror that is indeed implicit in all man's simpler relationships with the earth" and a utopian appreciation for the aesthetics of the city's architecture.[1] She says they were taken by a dream to leave the "cabbage patch" and enjoy beauties all of us are capable of enjoying in our more sensitive moments, "if the world will but go on getting richer." That they were returning from market or had come to meet each other was apparently inconceivable to West. Yet what is important about West's comments isn't her elitism or imperialist tendency to infer behaviour rather than materially prove it by speaking to people themselves, but the presence of peasants on the Stradun itself, whatever their reasons.

View of the Stradun in Dubrovnik, 1997.

Today I don't meet any peasants admiring architecture, only ones at work in the market. These old women look much like those in Zagreb; some are wearing plain black kerchiefs, black or dark blouses, and skirts, and they're selling plump red grapes, figs, oranges, limes, tomatoes, bay leaves, oleanders, and other flowers, which have all absorbed the lavish Dalmatian sun. On a wooden stool, one woman displays glass vials of rosemary, lavender, and thyme fluid. Starved for customers late in the afternoon, she calls out and holds up a bottle. I'm supposed to rub the stuff on my temples to cure my headaches. I see another elderly woman in a square, starched white kerchief, a white dress, and black leather slippers who is on her way home from a folklore event and cheerfully lets me take her picture. "Why not?" she laughs. "I'm all dressed up."

Such fleeting sights present a different Dubrovnik from West's. Now, while the city continues to age more or less naturally, not torn asunder by capitalism's renovations, modern tourism has re-inscribed traditional culture where it's languishing. But I feel that the relation between the city and people is tenuous, that they're only ghosts flitting around a place that doesn't tell their stories. For instance, while every tour guide mentions the large sixteen-sided reservoir and drinking fountain inside the Pile Gate, Velika Česma (part of one of the first city waterworks in Europe, 1444), none I've seen comments accurately on the live action around it. Men and boys are testing their balance on a foot-size stone with a gargoyle's face, which sticks out of the wall across from the cistern. One after another, they press their bellies against the wall and try to remove their T-shirts without falling off. I wonder if a long chain of days links these guys to the ones who started it God knows how long ago. This is a figure for life in Dubrovnik—an often unrecorded minutia of events subordinate to the urbane architecture itself.

As if in answer to this silence, a woman appears on a side street wearing a white trench coat and white clogs. Her black hair is cropped, her cheeks are rouged the colour of fresh blood, and her lashes are so heavily painted with mascara that her eyes are hidden. She portends something I haven't understood, adds a note of sobriety to the scene around her. She turns a corner and then is gone.

Dubrovnik's history is as turbulent as that of any Adriatic city, with one vital difference: through crafty diplomacy, its leaders were able to maintain its status as an independent republic, in practice if not by official decree. The balancing stone could also serve as a metaphor for this delicate, centuries-old political balancing act.

Dubrovnik was formerly called Ragusa, after the island of the same name just off the mainland (formerly Lausa, then Rausa). The island had been a haven for citizens of Epidaurus escaping rampaging bands of Avars and Slavs in the seventh century. During the same period, Slavs settled nearby on the wooded coast, which later provided the city with its final name (taken from the word *dubrava*, which means "glade"). The two groups merged, joined island to coast, and built walls. Today's city essentially arose from the ashes in 1292, when a fire tore through the mostly wooden buildings.

Dubrovnik became a world mercantile power on the sea and an important trading centre. As one historian writes,

> the period of greatest shipping activity began in 1450, and reached its peak between 1480 and 1600 ... Several sources report that there were 70 or 80 privately owned *navi da gabbia* (masthead ships, i.e., large ships with full-rigged masts) ... Venice had one of the largest merchant fleets in the Mediterranean; yet in 1559, for example, it had only 36 large sailing ships, while the Ragusan shipowners owned between 50 and 70 (the fluctuations reflect the loss of ships and the building of new ones) ... This merchant fleet was built only for trade, but the ships had to be well armed and strong enough to defend themselves against the North African corsairs.[2]

The city's affluence, importance, and prestige waned in the seventeenth century after the destruction caused by the earthquake of 1667, and the shift of trade towards the Americas. Yet its former prosperity assured that the word *argosy* (from Ragusa) became synonymous in English with "treasure ship." Ragusa also acquired a reputation for justice and science. It founded a medical service (1301), one of the first public pharmacies in Europe (1317), a shelter for the aged (1347), and a foundling hospital (1432). It also abolished slavery (1418) and established quarantine regulations against the Black Plague (1430).

The best view of the city is from its massive walls. So much is crowded within them that from up top, the city looks somewhat unplanned, partly since it's the amalgamation of many reconstructions over the centuries, resulting in a rich disparateness. Most recently, war damage has turned the roofs into a patchwork of earlier honey-coloured tiles and newer orange tiles from factories in France and Slovenia. A map shows a form of planning more clearly: the

View of the rooftops of Dubrovnik, 1997.

interior of the city consists mostly of civilian housing, while public and ecclesiastical buildings like the Rector's Palace, the Custom House, the Franciscan and Dominican monasteries, and the Cathedral are closest to the walls. In general, the city seems to have evolved in order to facilitate daily secular and business life by centralizing it.

The vicissitudes of time have left a jumble of marginal spaces no tourist guides promote: dead-end alleys, short cuts, weedy courtyards, and backyards that have become junkyards for old washing machines, sinks, bikes, car parts, TVs, cables, cement mixers, and broken tiles. I notice other spaces that the tourist books don't talk about either— the living spaces of the people themselves, extensions of residual people disconnected from Dubrovnik's tourism and its wealth. I see through

Reading in Dubrovnik, 1997.

open windows into little rooms where people are having coffee, playing cards, or leaning out in their undershirts, like one guy who's smoking and flicking a confetti of butts onto the street below.

Yet others are perfectly attuned to the city's cultured past. An old man in a starched cream shirt is reading by his window, a fountain pen and notebook beside him. Having spent so much with peasants, I've lost sight of the fact that there are elderly connoisseurs of art in Croatia, and certainly in Dubrovnik. Its literary heritage goes back before the mid-nineteenth-century Illyrian Movement, which made the city so important in the intelligentsia's collective imagination. The pastoral dramas and comedies of Marin Držić (1508–1567) are still performed today. Writers like Ivan Gundulić (1589–1638), author of

Osman, the epic poem about Turkish–Slav relations, wrote in a *štokavski* variant chosen later by the Illyrians as standard Croatian, even though (or because) it was closer to the Serbian.

In 1991, such dreams died. By the entrance of my landlady's house, a belt-high exploded shell now acts as a stand for geraniums. She leads me to the terrace and points to the mountain that looms over the entire region. "They shelled us from there," she says. Her rotund jolly face doesn't betray the fear of those days in 1991. Dubrovnik was pinned down and cut off. The Yugoslav Army's method of sporadic shelling, which would be used in the next four years to terrorize civilians in Croatia and Bosnia-Herzegovina, seemed to have begun here as well. Shells descended and smoke rose from the city. The world was much more outraged than it was about Vukovar, because Dubrovnik was known as a cultural city of the first rank, having been designated a UNESCO World Heritage Site in 1979.

"Even the Nazis didn't do this," she says.

In Croatia, cartoons depicted Serbs as primitive Balkan warriors in beards and capes who drank *šljivovica,* then scorched the land around them and planted signs that said, *This is Serbia*. But there was nothing funny for the people living in Dubrovnik who were at the mercy of a few Montenegrin and Serb soldiers in an invincible position in their bunkers. It would have been easy to decimate the city. They never did. They considered it a prize that would eventually be theirs, and so it was worth preserving. The bombardments were gratuitous and perverse, especially in light of the fact that few Serbs lived in the city and were threatened by the new so-called Ustaša regime. Moral outrage shielded the city as it didn't elsewhere in the Balkans. Dubrovnik escaped again.

West of the old town, the coast is indented by high-cliffed inlets, at the bottom of which are concrete platforms reachable by stairs that zigzag down. The water is a different shade of turquoise depending on the time of day. One dusk I see an owl perched on a flowering agave—a tree-like cactus that blooms once after thirty years and then dies. Somehow prescient, the owl has chosen this rare roost on which to orient itself. I watch it from the sidewalk above the stairs; far below, boulders like slumbering leviathans are dissipating in the darkening sea. I feel as if I've caught a moment when nature fleetingly holds sway in a human-saturated place, when an owl owns the dusk.

But like the agave, this moment doesn't last. The next day, I descend the same stairs to one of the terraces, where I'm confronted by a different and new ownership. Two older men, locals by the look of them, have decided to sit at the feet of a young woman, who is sun-tanning topless. One of the men, a husky fellow with white hair swept across his forehead like a glancing blow, sits on the step immediately below her, leaning back, his elbows almost against her feet. He and his friend could have sat anywhere else on this terrace but chose this spot instead. Furious, the woman gets up, covers herself, and leaves.

The men keep chatting as if nothing happened, actually seeming to get louder as she goes. More than a sign of machismo, this encounter reveals some locals' attitudes about property since the war. These men may number among those who spray-painted warnings to trespassers on the walls and stairs, even though such property isn't private. Brazen people tried to take over sections of abandoned hotel complexes or uninhabited villas, in some cases actually building walls so no one would dispute their "new" seafront property. Capitalism unloosed a post-communist predatory economics.

But not all of Dubrovnik is in such demand. On its seaward side, the streets become seedier, less tourist friendly; weeds grow out of cracks and gravel gathers in corners. A recently evicted bathtub sits in a dead-end street, and dozens of gaunt, malarial cats are scavenging for food.

Before I see her, I hear the clogs. The woman in the trench coat, her cheeks bloodied by rouge, passes me without looking. The opening in the wall where she goes leads to a post-apocalyptic space outside the town walls, a sort of gang turf. A ghetto blaster (the old term fits here) blasts out thrash music like a cement cracker. Graffiti are sprayed across the rocks and broken bottles litter the ground. A fridge is hooked to cords snaking from somewhere and there are a few plastic tables and chairs.

Squatting on the rocks like gargoyles are skinny brown boys around twelve years old, dragging on cigarettes. One kid is lying asleep on a flat rock. Steps coil steeply through the rocks to the water, where some boys are tossing a ball around. The woman, the only female present, leans against a rock, regally taking in this scene like a queen over her court. Everyone ignores her.

No source for any of this exists, no obvious origin or centre or will that designed this place, as if it were an accidental happening or, better, the woman's state of mind objectified. She hears my steps, looks at me for the first time and, seeing my camera, disappears down the stairs. Display and secrecy seem at odds within her. For me, she represents the state of a city still besieged by war, even though the war is over—damaged, slow to fully recover, and in need of attention.

I return to town. Soon I'm back among tourists, happily milling around the shops and sitting at cafés. I'm only two hundred yards north but in a different world. Most visitors will take away a different set of pictures and perpetuate Dubrovnik's urbane, cultured image. Undoubtedly deserved, this image melds into another, which is more sombre and more attuned to the country's other self since 1991, one I expect to revisit on my journey through the Dinaric interior.

▮▮▮ KRAJINA/HERZEGOVINA
The Zones

I'M DESTINED FOR KRAJINA AND WESTERN Herzegovina, the margins of Croat territory and identity. Such hard, mountainous, and windswept land seems antagonistic to life itself, but ironically, thousands died in major battles during the 1990s for the right to live there. If the Balkans are perceived as a cauldron of endemic ethnic hatred, the "Other" of the civilized democratic west, then some might call the Dinaric hinterland the Balkans of Croatia.

It's July 1999. The Gypsies I meet at Karlovac aren't affiliated with any side. They're trying to stay alive as usual. On their way to Duga Resa, they've stopped on the highway's turnoff to rest their horses— sad brown beasts pulling two wooden wagons. The first driver is a handsome man whose brown hair identically matches his animals'. He's taciturn, inscrutable, and stoic. "Life is harder than it used to be," he says. "People are different, not as friendly." He sucks on his cigarette. "Not at all."

"We live in Duga Resa today but who can say about tomorrow?" shrugs his wife. She's wearing a black-and-white polka-dot blouse, and no kerchief or jewellery of any kind. She's smiling and the kids are smiling, sitting among pillows, blankets, and bags.

They're not the people demonized in legends and despised in life. Except for her dark skin, the wife betrays little of her Gypsy blood— the storied look of a bespangled witch. I know of a woman in Brezje whose tale about a Gypsy woman's black magic is typical of peasant superstition. Ljubica insists she was hypnotized by a stranger who arrived at her door on the pretense of peddling curtains, but who eventually got into the house using her heavy melodious voice. Over a cup of *majčina dušica* (mother's soul) tea, the woman kept talking and talking about innocuous things, until finally, entranced, Ljubica began removing her rings, her earrings, and her chain. She handed them over one by one, knowing something was wrong but persuaded by a strong will that seemed to reach deep inside her. The woman finished her tea and disappeared down the road. Were it not for her husband, who arrived later and was spared the woman's powers, Ljubica says she would never have gotten back her treasures.

While the people I just met might not always walk the straight and narrow, they don't possess black magic; they don't own much of anything. They just look defeated. For them, the last decade of the twentieth century posed the added problem of a new underclass of refugees from parts of Croatia and Bosnia-Herzegovina who sought new homes. All were Gypsies of a kind and all knew the zone mentality of homelessness and instability, willingly or not. They either came from areas where their identities were assailed, or they were born into that situation. The arrival of so many new refugees explains the increased hostility towards his people that the Gypsy driver mentioned. More than just representing contemporary demographic change, refugees also index the life often led in this territory, this place of human movement and isolation; of military nomadism determined by the tectonic clash of empires, cultures, and religions: the Christian west versus the Islamic east; of pastoral nomadism determined by the vagaries of sheep. Until the late 1980s, shepherds from Lika still drove their animals into Prigorje early every spring before returning in the summer. People would rise in the mornings to the sight of sheep on their empty unplowed fields.

I see no signs of this life today. After Karlovac, the road starts to wind like a drunk on its way to the coast. *Gostionicas* appear—some new or refurbished, others gutted and abandoned. Piglets and lambs turn on spits in big steel barbecues. Before, Gypsies used to stop their wagons at these spots to sell copper pots and wicker baskets, sometimes uncaging muzzled, mangy bears so tourists would pay for photographs with them.[1]

Beside *gostionicas* or along the highway at convenient stopping points, peasant women sell cheese, honey, *šljivovica*, and *loza* under sun umbrellas. I speak to one tall vendor of around fifty who has black permed hair and a long masculine face, dark and chiselled. "You're in Kordun," she says in a deep, straight-ahead voice.[2] "This is Croat land. You still got your Serbs around, see there, those women at that table are Serbs. And those houses with the façades, the nice ones, those too. Most of them left."

"You talk to them?"

"Hell no, we don't get together. None of that."

"What's going to happen between Croats and Serbs here?"

"Nothing's gonna happen. They'll live and we'll live. They'll be fine if they leave us alone. We got an army now."

Images of my grandfather's last moments come to me. A few months before my father's birth, he died here somewhere in a broken building or bunker after he and his Domobran compatriots got drunk and were ambushed by Partisans. He was asleep, and couldn't be woken or was left behind, according to my uncle, who was forever embittered by this loss. I know the story from a man in Mala Gorica, who was there that evening but who died before I could speak to him. I'd like to have heard and watched him tell the story, to detect whether the crime my uncle accused him and the others of would assume a form on his face.

I pause for a second. What am I supposed to feel in this moment? I can't claim some new bond to my grandfather simply because I visited the region where he died. I've learned nothing new about the little I know—that he loved life, loved company, loved to drink, was good (they say), was strong, worked hard, and resembled me physically. Looking around, I don't see a particular place in which to invest my

The Catholic church destroyed by Četnici during World War One (Lika), 1999.

feelings. Instead, I feel empty as I contemplate the brevity of his life, its uncertain value, and the lives he might have held together if given the chance. I wish I could say I sense his thoughts sent ahead once, and that he felt me looking back. But I can't. I get the feeling he was hooked too securely in his present for such dreams and, like the people he grew up with, was too practical.

I drive on, past Slunj where the river Korana white-waters under the town's houses, past the Plitvice Lakes and Waterfalls, a UNESCO World Natural Heritage site, and then into the rolling open spaces of Lika. Here, crags and stones nudge their noses out of the meadows; here are fields dusted by purple and yellow flowers, pockets of pines, and willows with light silvery leaves. The dark-blue Plješevica Mountains rise on the left and then the road splits at Korenica; the one I take is the narrower, empty truck route to Knin, which winds steeply up through the Krbava Mountains.

The temperature starts to drop. The land opens up again as meadows run up to the road, occasionally marked by rickety wood fences. There's a forlorn bus stop, but not a single house for miles.

Like a lot of Lika, this plateau is sheep grazing land, open and close to the sky, yet no animals are in sight.

The church at Bunić makes me stop. The roof is gone; a tree grows up the church's left flank and tufts of grass grow out of the stone, resembling bullet holes from where I stand. This church is haunting.

The hamlet is no more than an empty collection of houses on a turn in the road. Going down an alley, I notice some chickens, a demolished house with *Hrvatska kuća* (Croat house) graffitied on it, and across from it a little dwelling with a new coat of whitewash beside a dilapidated barn. I get out and knock on the door.

Behind a smudged window in the door, the old man looks scared. He keeps repeating, "The lady of the house isn't home, the lady of the house isn't home." Because he's shouting, he can't hear a word I say.

When I'm about to give up, an old woman comes from the back yard. She's breathless. Her hands tremble as she moves a stool for me. She has greying black hair, sad dark eyes, and wears two kerchiefs around her neck, one she probably just took off. "Here you are, sir," she says in feigned casualness. "And this one for me, a fine place to sit." She wedges a broken chair onto some rocks around the tree in the front. Her name is Katica and the old man with the round wrinkled head and a yellow fang sticking from his mouth is Milan. She's Croat and he's Serb. "The church was like that when we came. My husband knows," she says in answer to my question.

"Right, right," he mumbles unclearly through his gums. "Četnici did that in World War One."

"The church is still here and so are you," I say.

"We're here, but what do we have? Look around, I ask you," she answers. "We lived in our apartment in Lički Osik for thirty-six years and then there was Oluja and then we came here, where my husband was born. I jumped from the balcony. The Cetnici said they were going to kill me. Now we're alone in an empty village and…" Her voice breaks off. She looks down and smoothens her wrinkled dress.

They drink and cook with water that she transports from a well three kilometres away, but they use rainwater to wash. The European organization ECHO redid the house and the couple gets twenty dollars a month from the Red Cross. This is their only source of support since they receive nothing from the Croatian government, despite repeated

Katica and Milan outside their house in an
abandoned hamlet in Lika, 1999.

requests. It seems that Serbs living in Jasenovac get benefits that Serbs (and Croats) in more remote parts of the country don't, perhaps because the government became conscious of appearing ethnically discriminatory in the eyes of the west.

"I go to town for cigarettes and things, if a good soul stops for me." She points to a puppy in the yard. "I got him from a man in town. I begged him to give me the dog so we would have something at least." How will they feed it if they can hardly feed themselves, I wonder. Yet when I meet them, in this, the United Nations' International Year of the Old Person, they've already survived out here for four years.

In Knin stands a statue of a Croat soldier with his arms in the air, the right hand holding a machine gun, two fingers on the left hand in a V for victory. Commemorating the Oluja offensive in 1995, the statue brings to mind the war-torn history of the Krajina region. The Vojna Krajina (military frontier) was established in the sixteenth century during Hapsburg rule to repulse Ottoman attacks into the empire. The frontier was essentially a series of forts, garrisoned by German mercenaries and Croats, then by Orthodox (and some Catholic) Vlachs or Morlachs who were eventually freed from serfdom by the Hapsburgs in exchange for military service. The ethnic identity of these settlers became a contentious issue during the struggle by their descendants, Krajina's Serbs, to secede from Croatia and join a greater Serbia. But as historians note, ethnic categories didn't mean the same thing in the late twentieth century as they did in the sixteenth. Notably, even as recently as the mid 1800s, Josip Jelačić led his partly Serb *graničari* into battles during a time of rising pan-Slavism.

I arrive in Knin after a drive through the last tails of the imposing Velebit Mountains, which thunder southward and into the interior. This is beautiful terrain that alternately opens into pale grassy valleys and then shuts like pincers, forming deep fjord-like chasms. A buzzard floats high above. Dozens of houses along the way have been destroyed, their black, empty windows staring vacantly at the road, looking like headstones in a giant graveyard. Here and there are occupied homes, but they are usually distant from each other as in the North American prairies. Most of the Serbs here and in Knin left for Bosnian-Serb territory and Serbia proper, where they imagined a future.

Knin belongs to Croatia but is a pure slice of Yugoslavia. It's a dreary railway junction connecting Zagreb to the Dalmatian coast, and its apartment blocks are blackened, stained, and graffitied (one in English reads, *No dope, no hope*). The new Croatia hasn't come to Knin.

On the hill above the city is a fortress originally built by King Zvonimir (ruler between 1075 and 1089) and then rebuilt by the Ottomans in the sixteenth century and the Venetians in the eighteenth. The first four workers in the post office, all Croats, don't know who built it, but then the fifth gets it right. The others are embarrassed, but they can't really be blamed since they've only moved here recently from other territories in the former Yugoslavia.

I wander into the railway station in search of a toilet. The restaurant is empty and the waiter is behind the bar, washing glasses. "There's no one here," I say in Croatian.

"You're the first guest," he answers in English. "I got more comin tomorrow. Beeg wedding party, two hundred guests, so I gotta set up." His name is Johnny and he worked on Carnival Cruise Lines for twelve years before coming here. He dunks the glasses once into the soapy sink, then lets the tap water run over them for a second before lining them up on a tray. "You Amereecuns and Canadeeuns don unerstan Croatia," he says after I tell him my purpose in coming. "You don know nothin. I know your dad he's from here but you don know nothin." He makes an unflattering remark about Mila Mulroney, referring to the Serb wife of former Canadian Prime Minister Brian Mulroney; by doing nothing, he says, Mulroney and other western leaders essentially condoned Serb attacks carried out under the guise of the Yugoslav Army.

"Those destroyed houses you saw were Croatian houses. Everything Croatian. You gotta write that. But nevermind, I don mean no disrespect. You're gonna sit now and eat a fine meal. Everything you want, my wife she an excellent cook."

I look around. The neon lights are shining brightly, the TV is booming to an empty room, and the tablecloths are stained. Instead of a picture of Tito on the wall, there's a *šahovnica*. In Knin, it's as good a place for a meal as any.

I drive into the vast Neretva River valley, which lies between mountains near the Bosnia-Herzegovina border in southern Dalmatia. A huge patchwork quilt has been flung over the valley—vegetable gardens, orchards, wheat and cornfields—everything fed by canals off the river's arms. I see houses right on the water, concrete embankments, docks reeling in dories, fruit stands lining the highway, and watermelons sprayed with river water pumped through fat hoses.

The border is at Metković. Friendly but glum border guards thoroughly search my trunk. There are no formal gates to drive through, no exchange offices or restaurants—just some men on a dusty road jammed with trucks in the heat. Stark mountainous hills threaten the road and houses all along are smashed to pieces with spiteful vengeance while a few are perfectly intact and inhabited. Swinging off long cables are two Jeeps being transported by military helicopters. I see the rusted shell of a an old Fiat impaled on a tree five feet off the ground. A few kilometres west is the village of Medjugorje, which has become a shrine for Catholics and Christian pilgrims since the Virgin Mary allegedly began appearing to six teenagers in 1982. Looking around, I see how such a hard region could have inspired religious devotion or, some might say, fanaticism.

Brightening the bare hills, the jade Neretva shows up now and again. Dazzling yellow-and-blue birds flit across the road. Mostar is beautiful as well, yet it's reduced in places to ugly rubble. The old quarter is mostly preserved, but the closer you get to the main drag that leads in from the highway, still called by its old name, Bulevar Narodne Revolucije (Boulevard of National Revolution), the more damage there is. This was the line dividing Croats on the west from Muslims on the east during the war of 1993. Buildings on the Muslim side are the worst off, jagged ruins pointing skyward like petrified teeth from a giant desert jawbone.

I meet two men on a temporary crossing over the Neretva where Tito's Bridge used to stand—one a Muslim, the other a Serb. This is a lucky meeting and a symbolic one. Both men hang onto the idealism of Yugoslav *Bratstvo i Jedinstvo*, which still appeals to some in Mostar and Bosnia-Herzegovina. "Of course we're still friends," says the Muslim, Fuad Ačkar, a slim man of fifty with white hair and a dark-brown face carved with lines. "We were before and now we still are. The war didn't kill that," he says.

At a café, his Serb friend offers me homemade *loza* from a plastic mickey he carries around as a sample from the private reserve he sells. When the waiter arrives, I order an Ožujsko and everyone laughs. "We don't sell that here," the waiter says, meaning they don't sell Croat beer. I feel piqued but not enough to make a fuss. Clearly there's some animosity left over from the war. Let them laugh; after all, their lives are in shambles like Mostar itself.

Fuad's marriage broke up too. Although his wife and son live in Denmark, he returned without them. "Herzegovina was too much in my heart. It called me back." The real reason is unclear; he broke off relations with his son, who called him a traitor to the family. He has no job and lives off odd work and handouts. Through everything, he remains a good sort. "I will be friends with everyone. And I still have Croat friends but I felt more aggression from them than from Serbs. I can't speak to many of them now. I'm for peace only. Yugoslavia was my country. 'Hej Slaveni' was my anthem," he says, shrugging apologetically. "I will die now, this moment, if Tudjman were shot and people could live normally."

I'm about to go, so I ask his Serb friend what his name is. He doesn't want to give it to me at first. "What?! Why are you like this now?" says Fuad, raising his arms.

"I don't want to, that's all."

"Oh come on, don't be like that."

He agrees to do it in the end, writing, *TOPLICA STANKOVIĆ.* *SERB.* He underlines the last part emphatically. They laugh.

Later, I head to the old bridge that gave Mostar its name. It was blown up by Croatian artillery on November 9, 1993, four years to the day after the Berlin Wall came down and fifty-five years after Kristallnacht. Such a primitive act was timed with considerable calculation. The bridge was a single stone span built by an architect called Hajrudin in 1566. The legend that grew up around its construction is concisely related by Paul Blanchard—and no longer correctly, as it turns out.

> The first span collapsed, and the Sultan, furious, sent for the architect and warned him that, if the next one did not hold, Hajrudin would pay with his head. When at last the bridge was finished the architect was nowhere to be found; certain that it would not stand, he had fled to Bijelo Polje. The townspeople sought him out and bore him to the Sultan, by whom he was

Remains of the old bridge in Mostar, 1999.

duly congratulated. Four centuries later the bridge is
still standing.[3]

On the way down, I negotiate streets paved by river stones locked
in concrete. Minarets pierce the blue sky and grey limestone roofs slant
low down like caps pulled over eyes. A shopkeeper is hosing down the
sidewalk. Only one store I see offers traditional folk items like copper
coffee pots, pipes, carpets, and leather shoes with curled toes called
opanci (to hold when you shit, Croats say). In the shade across from
a mosque, three men are sitting on the ground in the shade drinking
beer, bottles fallen around them like bowling pins. Construction
workers who are smoking and chatting, greet me as I go by. Some

Croats I know are rabidly convinced all Muslims are lazy but the heat today would silence such critics.

A temporary bridge, where the old one used to stand, spans the Neretva. The original stones are assembled on the western side, having been pulled out in 1997. On the day I visit, they're still waiting to be reassembled.[4]

Underneath the terraced restaurants on an escarpment, an old man has stuck a rock on his fishing rod and is waiting. The Neretva roils thickly past, sprinkled with bits of unwholesome refuse from the sewers, its twisting surface hinting at currents that have sucked swimmers to their deaths. Further down, kids are leaping into the river from a rock three metres high. When the bridge was intact, young men would dive off it one after another in glorious sequences.

Azir Skreža has his shirt off and is enjoying a smoke. He assures me there are fish in the Neretva and that they can even be eaten. He's at peace here, but when I ask him about his Croat neighbours, he growls, "Those damn Croats, damn Croats."

I drive west across the former front into the Croat sector of Mostar. Right away, I feel I'm back in Zagreb because the houses are grander and fronted by tree-lined boulevards. In contrast to the Muslim side, only a few demolished houses testify to the fighting. This situation results from the lesser beating taken by the Croats and money for reconstruction pumped in by the Croatian government in Zagreb.

Near the top of the district, I park the car and climb a steep driveway into a grassy yard overlooking all of Mostar. An imposing vista opens up—a fresco of orange and grey roofs, ruthlessly barren mountains to the east, and bunkers on the tops of the mountain instead of churches, grey like the rocks themselves.

The man sitting outside has never had a Canadian show up in his yard, requesting that a plastic bottle be filled with water. He's strong and compact like a fullback, with a similar delivery. "OK, but have a beer if you want." When he comes back we stand in the yard over the view. I tell him I met a Muslim and a Serb in town, and was at the site of the old bridge. He has nothing negative to say about the other ethnic groups. "That's war. There was fighting all around here. We lost things too."

"What's it like now?"

"We got our police and they got theirs. I had some friends before, but now...," he pauses. "Things stand differently. We're better off this way. We're not the same people."

"Who built those?"

"The bunkers? The Austrians built them, I think. I'm not really sure. My neighbour, he's the one to ask, a real professor of history. Just a moment." He goes to the next yard and comes back accompanied by a short, balding man wearing steel-rimmed glasses, who introduces himself as Josip Glibić, a civil engineer who works for a Slovenian company in Libya. Our host brings out more chairs while his wife pours out jiggers of *šljivovica*. A few neighbours drop by and listen in. Without intending to, I've created a small communal event, a reason to get together.

"He's right," Glibić says. "The Austrians did build those bunkers when they took over from the Turks in 1878. I don't need to tell you that this area has long been contested and we Croats have sometimes been at peace, but often at war. Through it all we have managed to keep our identity. This is what Yugoslavia as an idea could not permit nor has ever permitted. Even though we are not part of Croatia in Herzegovina, we are all Croats in our hearts. What is now Slavonia, at other times called Pannonia, was divided from Dalmatia for hundreds of years, yet Slavonians and Dalmatians are all Croats in their hearts. You cannot artificially control this by changing the name of the country."

"Do you feel this more strongly here?"

"If you mean that because we are outside we feel more attachment to our motherland, you are right. Herzegovinans are proud patriots." This is particularly the case with the Croat diaspora who are the most distant in time and space, and are therefore more likely to find solace and meaning in the symbols of Croat identity.

"Should the bridge be put back together?"

"It is not a question of should. It *must* be put back together. And I hope they do it soon."

Glibić seemed wise enough to know the inevitable consequences of ethnic-centred policies of a government so far away in Zagreb. Such governments change, and with them the hands that protect. If there is a nationalist, irredentist yearning among Herzegovinan Croats, a narcissism of minor difference that ended the arc of its illogic with the bombing of an old Muslim bridge, it would have to be tempered by such reasonableness as Glibić's in order for Croats here to actually thrive. It could happen, but not right away. Out of the barren, unforgiving ground to which living things clung like barnacles on a sheer cliff, extremism seemed to flourish too easily, a Medjugorje of soul whereby the tears of Mary were perversely commensurate with falling shells.

12 ■ ISTRIA
The Gentle Climate

FROM THE SOUTHERNMOST, MARGINAL REGION claimed by Croats, I travel to the one furthest west. The impostor of a highway from Prigorje to Istria twists narrowly through the mountains and forests of Gorski Kotar, where vistas open up onto valleys given over to farming, where roadhouses like the ones in Kordun roast yet more whole pigs and lambs, and where tiny dwellings like those in Zagorje hug the road. The highway eventually widens high above Rijeka, the largest port in Croatia, and takes me near one of the country's most popular tourist resorts, and a favourite during the Austro-Hungarian Empire, Monaco-like Opatija.

The Istrian peninsula is a combination of hilly, even mountainous, terrain in the interior and rolling flatlands that slide in places right into the sea, unlike most of the Adriatic coast. Instead of bunkers on barren rock in a violent fault zone, there are towns and villages encircling the tips of steep hills. If such design speaks about the history of the Istrian interior, it tells about the collective resistance to invaders like the Turks while the region was simultaneously under Venetian rule, not about nineteenth-century Austrian imperialism or late twentieth-century ethnic hatred. Today it tells about the Istrians' somewhat isolated but peaceful coexistence, which characterized Istria ever since the arrival of settlers from Turkey, Greece, and the rest of the Balkans in the seventeenth century during a post-plague repopulation period on the peninsula. Istria has never been ethnically divided like the Krajina or Slavonia, although the differing demographics between coast and interior (i.e., Venetian and Slavic) eventually led to conflicts between Italy and Yugoslavia.

When I see a cloak of orange building blocks draped over the peak of a hill, I turn in and drive the steep road to the top. This is Motovun. I park the car outside the eighteenth-century gate and walk up the cobblestoned street that leads to the fourteenth-century ramparts that once protected the old town. I pass an open garage filled with wooden bas-reliefs, dozens of them displayed on the concrete floor and along the walls. The man who carves them is staining one. "I'm an artist with no inspiration. So I'm doing this instead," he says. "It makes me feel productive."

I look at all the reliefs around him. Some epic ones, three yards long, depict traditional Istrian life—farmers and horses ploughing, backgrounded by stylized geometrical villages and mountain ranges, while other carvings show women hoeing, villages, flowers, and trees. The work is detailed, delicate, showing deft talent. "But you are productive."

"Ah come on, the last one I did was two weeks ago. I didn't even start a new carving. The only reason there's so many here is because no one's buying. I can't get inspired in this situation."

"They're beautiful. Why aren't people buying?"

"No tourists this season. Even during the war years, it was normal. No one has deep enough pockets." His name is Toni Djermadi, a tanned wisp of a man with holes in place of his front teeth, whose family arrived from Medjumorje in northern Croatia in 1964. He's not peasant stock so his carvings aren't based on personal experience. "They're fantasy, nothing more. I dream worlds into life." Yet like other good artists, he's realizing the truth of a way of life, using linden wood to get at the spirit of a world now gone. The smaller carvings verge on kitsch because they don't capture a totality of experience, and they look so obviously on sale. Djermadi is in it for the money but he's an artist as well, someone for whom selling is confirmation of his talent and purpose. Now that he's not earning anything, his confidence is shaken. He also connects his financial problems with the country's, and finds in "liberty" an abstract concept with no substance.

"We have freedom but we're hungry."

I walk the rest of the way to the top. In an archway hang great slabs of unevenly shaped stone inscribed by Glagolitic writing. Through the gate I can see flat stretches of country and distant dustings of orange on hills. The forests surrounding Motovun were once protected by the Venetians as a major source of wood for their ships, as occurred elsewhere along the Adriatic.

Throughout history, foreigners had come to little Motovun when the locals didn't want them. In a year when there is finally peace and freedom, however, they've stopped coming. While Djermadi deplored the lack of visitors, the hazy stillness of the afternoon has put the town peacefully to sleep, and I circulate alone, happily.

The owner of the place outside Rovinj where I stay for the night comes out of his cellar the next morning with a cloudy glass of homemade wine. To refuse would insult him so I drink what I can, appreciating this gesture of hospitality so common among Croats. But there are limits to what I can take in the morning and I ashamedly leave a partly full glass on his table. Years of visits to friends and family taught me to hold off draining my drinks until just before leaving, unless I wanted them promptly filled. It took me years to learn this, and even now I find myself leaving neighbours' homes in mid-morning with the "zap on my head," so to speak.

I say goodbye and drive to my next destination. The interior of Istria is highly elusive, and the roads are like capillaries spreading in different directions. I know my journey through Croatia is coming to an end, so I feel rather given to the seeming directionlessness of this network. I could travel all day, not experience much of note, but still feel I spent the day well. The way winds through small settlements where I stop periodically for directions. If you're in Istria, that's a pleasure in itself. Eventually, I pull up beside a rock wall where some locals are chatting underneath a willow tree.

"The White Friars?" asks a man wearing a blue tank top, something like a summer work uniform in Istria. "No problem. But come on out first, have a rest."

"Where you from?" his wife asks.

"Canada. My dad's from near Samobor," I say, using my usual entry code.

"Canada! But he talks our language, doesn't he?"

"Sure does," her husband agrees. "I was in Samobor once. 1974 I think. Nice place."

"How 'bout a drink?" she asks.

"Right, I'll bring out the wine," he says.

"No, no, beer's fine, half a glass!" I tell him sharply. "If you have beer, I mean."

"Sure we got beer. Right, go get the beers, and glasses too," he tells her. "You're our first Canadian," he says, whacking me on the back.

"Nice to be here. Friendly people." I apprise them of Captain Mile in Pupnatska Luka, as a way of learning about them, and about the Istrian temperament.

"You won't find that here," a neighbour states categorically. He is a paunchy man, also in a blue tank top, who is settled on a moped. "An Istrian will never treat anyone that way. Istria is more laid-back than other parts," he adds.

"Do you feel Croat or Istrian?"

"Well, we're all Croats. But we belong here," says the guy on the moped. I'd heard that, except for two districts, the peninsula had resisted the political advances of nationalist parties. According to the 1991 census, twenty percent of Istrians listed their nationality as Istrian. These people sound like moderates who are proud of their country, yet attached intimately to their region. But I haven't detected anything aggressively insular so far—that combination of proud self-promotion and insecurity produced by a region's separation from a cultural and political centre.

They invite me to lunch. I can eat now, I can eat later, I can have more beer. But I'm off to see the White Friars in Sveti Petar u Šumi (St. Peter in the woods), so I thank them and leave. Following their directions, I take the first left fifty metres down by a bocce court, then travel through farming country and rolling terrain. Now and again a rock wall or outcropping of stone or herd of goats reminds me I'm still near the sea.

Sveti Petar is a sprawling collection of houses centred around a church and three crosses. The middle one is a crucifix and is built in such a way that the sun rising in the east spends much of the day behind or above Christ's head, giving the effect of a halo.

The White Friars belong to the Order of the Apostle Paul, which disappeared in Croatia during the reign of Joseph II in the Hapsburg Empire. The two fathers have come from Poland, where the Order still has a few faithful, to sow the seeds anew in Istria. Father Christofer is Polish, but he is fluent in Croatian. He wears a white robe, a white belt, and a rosary. When I ask him to explain the differences between his order and others, he couches his answer in history. The order was established in 1225, he says, and formally in 1250. The first White Friars lived in the forests above the Danube in Hungary. But today, I ask, what is specifically unique about them? He tells me that the Apostles established Croatia's first university in the sixteenth century. Their rosaries are comparable to the Dominicans' in style.

His answers may be telling. While constructive and noble in its way, the enterprise seems abstractly disconnected from the present; most young Croats are unlikely to embrace religion the way elderly women do. Attracting the young, of course, is one reason for the White Friars' arrival in Croatia. Yet I can't help but wonder whether their work will ever spread significantly beyond this county, or whether it will become exemplary of an insularity Istria seems to lack.

Knowing what I do about Croats' general attitude about men of the cloth, the White Friars have work ahead of them. The man who pointed out to me that the Friars' car wasn't there when I first arrived also dead-panned, "It looks like they're doing their banking." If we spoke more, he might have added that Sveti Petar u Šumi is notable as one of the districts that did support the HDZ, and that the political climate of the 1990s helped reinvigorate religious nostalgia. Just a few kilometres away, the ground seems less fertile for such an endeavour.

I'm running out of gas on the way to Šušnjevica, the heart of the Romanian population in Istria. I've come off a main road not far from Hum, the self-declared smallest town in the world, and started down a stretch of gravel that splits like a terrible schizophrenic. There's no way to know which road is right, since none appear on the map and there are no signs. To the north are imposing mountains and to the south are open spaces rumpled by hills.

The car's empty light comes on at the moment when slate-brown cows block the road. This is indeed a rare sight belonging to an earlier time, even in contemporary peasant communities, since livestock are normally chained inside barns. I get out to talk to the old cowherd. He's tall and lean and healthy looking, like most people who spend a lifetime working outside. His narrow Modigliani-like face is solemn. On his back is a wicker basket, clutched in his big hand are a scythe and a rake, and hooked in his belt is a small sickle, maybe to cut mistletoe and other herbs for his homemade brandy, *biska*. He points ahead to a clearing in the trees where his cows will graze. So accustomed are they to grazing in this pasture that they trundle on ahead while he stays behind talking to me. "I can't help you," he says. "I have no tractor, no gasoline. I live a simple life," he shrugs.

I ask him about his family. He looks at me, pausing, then answers, "That was before. Now they are my family," he says, nodding towards the pasture. A trace of a smile flashes up from somewhere, and he nods and follows his cows.

I go back to the car. On the left is a thatched stone barn and below the road a clutch of sheep in a glade. The scene is about as bucolic as any I've seen in Croatia. Once again, I'm struck by the beauty of these old places, by people's choices of the most attractive settings in which to build their lives.

I drive further. The road eventually takes me to Šušnjevica. When I arrive, I'm disappointed to learn that the Romanian presence has run out of gas too. One old man tells me he's Romanian. "Lots of ush here are," he whistles, "but not many people talk the old tongue anymore. I knew shum words, forgot all of them." The young guys on the road point me to a big house belonging to the businessman and mechanic Josip Kontuš. Kontuš is a polite, friendly man who offers me a seat and a beer in his dining room. Speaking in low, formal tones, he explains that most of the original Romanian settlers in this part of Istria spoke a Romanian dialect, not the original of the motherland.

Thatched barn near Šušnjevica (Istria), 1999.

The oldest people who still knew the language have died, and many others have emigrated to New York. The Romanian presence is dying out. But there are efforts to keep it alive.

"The Romanian ambassador to Croatia was here last week. He sat in the same chair you're sitting in now." Later I contact Constantin Girda, and he tells me that while Romanian culture is dwindling, some locals do speak a variant of the language, what he calls a "family dialect." Possibly a product of the Roman colonization of the Balkans, this Istro-Romanian dialect, a Latin language very similar to Romanian, is said to be distinguishable from other variants spoken by people scattered throughout the Balkans. The original identity and origin of the Istro-Romanians is uncertain. Historians generally believe they began arriving from the fifteenth century onwards after the Ottoman invasions. They may have come from what is presently Romania or from elsewhere in the Balkans, in which case they would almost certainly have been Vlachs who had progressed gradually westward in search of pastoral land (or had been deported or resettled into frontier zones by the Turks, and then had dispersed on their own into Venetian or Hapsburg lands).[1]

Efforts to maintain some form of cultural infrastructure and connection with Romanian heritage proper are continuing. It strikes me as we're talking that Istria is a suitable place for these kinds of efforts because there's no worry of extreme nationalism veering them in a different direction. Unlike these assimilated Romanians, Croats who have immigrated to the far corners of the world have, for the most part, clung tenaciously to their language and culture. Were they disposed because of their unique and unsettled history, in which they were perpetually divided, to such loyalty, such longing for a homeland? Or has not enough time passed for them to lose touch? My ties to Croatia are strong, but my future grandkids might feel differently. Too often have I seen even first-generation children of Croat immigrants absolutely concentrated on belonging in their parents' adopted environments, buying into commercial dress codes, behaviour, products, etc. What will Croat mean to them in the future? I can't claim to know.

■

I make my way to the coast of Istria, where its Italian minority still lives. The Italians controlled much of Istria until the end of World War Two, and while many left, others have stayed to this day. Even now there are old people who speak little Croatian.

The city of Pula boasts the sixth-biggest existing Roman amphitheatre and an industrial harbour. Only the former is reason for coming here now, but for the Austrians in the 1860s the harbour was a major naval port, dockyard, and arsenal. Following Dante, who reportedly stayed in Pula, James Joyce taught English to naval officers at the Berlitz school from October 1904 to March 1905. As one writer points out (partly incorrectly), this was the period when "three languages, Italian, German, and *Serbian*, could be heard on any street corner."[2] For Joyce's wife, Nora, Pula was a

> "Queer old place," and she urged Joyce to finish his book and get rich so they could live in Paris; she even began to study French to prepare herself for that pleasure. To Joyce, Pola [sic] was "a back-of-God-speed place," in fact, "a naval Siberia." The whole

Waterfront buildings in Rovinj, 1999.

Istrian peninsula he dismissed as "a long boring place
wedged into the Adriatic, peopled by ignorant Slavs
who wore little red caps and colossal breeches."[3]

I travel to Rovinj. It's a pure slice of Italy: tall waterfront buildings
that form a fresco of faded tangerine and yellow, little white and red
shuttered windows, and hundreds of clotheslines. On summer nights,
Rovinj is humming with life. Even the market stays open well past
dark. A guy with scissors stops me in the street, cuts out my profile in
paper, and then asks for five bucks. There's a shop selling the same
sort of factory-made wood objects available in Dolac and other markets
across the country, as well as thousands of other curios—whistles,
toys, chessboards and pieces, bocce balls, cigarette boxes, stools,
tamburicas, baseball bats. The oldest streets are so slick and roughly
cobbled I have trouble getting down them. There are alleys leading to
people's front porches, which are stone slabs right on the water. Now
and again the sewer's stink mixes with the smell of the sea.

In all the streams of people, the music, and the noise, I nearly miss
the two little legs poking out from a pile of plastic and cardboard.

The face—nearly hidden in the dark where the lights don't reach—is wizened, hollowed by shadows. This old woman is going to spend the night here. She's the only street person I've ever seen in this country. Others must share my surprise because they stop and look at her too. "Yeah, she's always there," a female vendor tells me in a surly voice.

The next morning, I find her across the street beside her box of cheeses. It's a typical thirty-five-degree summer day, but she's wearing a ski jacket. There's money in the plastic lunch bag she's clinging to, though I can't imagine anyone risking her cheese. Because she has no teeth left, I can hardly pick out a word she says. But I can understand the misery—the gurgling, choking anger and tears, which are almost comical—as she tells me of a man somewhere in her past, not her husband, who drove her to this state. If she claims any form of justice it comes from strangers who listen to her story, give her a few kunas, and then leave.

But such desperation is rare in Istria, according to my experience. On my last day I meet a woman who better exemplifies the Istrian personality and life. Ana is head cook at Rovinj's hospital, a slim, attractive woman in her forties who has adopted Istria as her homeland, even though she was born in Slovenia.

"There are three Istrias," she tells me, "based on the pigmentation and properties of the soil. Rovinj is part of Red Istria, which has very fertile but porous earth, excellent for Malvasian sweet wine. In Red Istria we await the full moon before digging out garlic cloves, so they won't shrivel all winter. White Istria is in the northwest where the soil is lighter. The grey area in the northeast we call Čičarija."

We're examining a map at her neighbour's place, where I'm staying for the night. "In Red Istria we have two harvests—the only region in all Croatia that does. Our climate is gentle, like our people, and no snow falls here. Farmers follow the moon to tell them when exactly to plant the next crop. The first potatoes are planted in February and are ready around July."

Despite her love for Istria, Ana's standard of living has gone down considerably since Croatia's independence. "I still have my old country in my heart. There is poison here we will get rid of." She's reflective for a moment. "But Istria is far away from the politics in Zagreb—far away in ideas, maybe not in kilometres. In Istria, we live three times better than in America. And they have no idea."

My journey ends on this note of peaceful confidence about a region and its way of life. I find it comforting to finish here, as if the very best of the Croat temperament were concentrated in this small peninsula. Whether through good luck, the absence of bad, or fortunate social relations established long ago, Istria has avoided the bloodletting evident at times elsewhere in Croatia.

■ CONCLUSION

BECAUSE I CONCENTRATED ON CROATIA'S DYING traditional ways in a closing chapter of its history and on my own experiences in the present, much of the rest is left out of focus, like the background of a photo. Were I to "photograph" this Croatia, I would start by showing more of its contemporary urban life (not all of it assignable to the usual snarl of congestion, bad air, and so on): the social and class nuances of vibrant café culture in the old cities' august streets, on busy avenues where buses roar by and cars are parked up on the sidewalks, book-ending the tables, in smaller towns and in villages where posh establishments have risen out of corn fields; I would "capture" the casual cadence and atmosphere of the cities; the landscape of boutiques, discos, restaurants, hotels, villas, yachts, luxury cars, tourist attractions, and sports complexes, which signal the hedonistic prosperity some are enjoying here, not all of it gotten illegally; heavily made-up but beautiful girls prancing like princesses through their worlds; shorn young guys pimp rolling through theirs; occasional longhairs—rockers and artistes; the arrogant train station guard who took my passport and made me wait an hour for a stamp while he sipped espresso in his office; hulking policemen who bark orders through car windows; the smells of the streets: diesel, Chanel, roast chestnuts, frying garlic, the stale sea of the big ports; the sounds as well: the hoots of trams, steel wheels, chug of tour boats, waspish outboards, forlorn whistles of trawlers; if I photographed this Croatia I would show the hundreds of drama, music, art, film, and folklore festivals, business and science fairs, as well as Croatia's many galleries, bookstores, theatres, schools and universities, so no one could doubt the talent and competence in this small country; and I would take people inside Croatia's sports culture, from local soccer matches watched by men leaning over wire fences around pitches, drinking beer and looking out for "wanted men" from the neighbouring village's team, to informal water-polo games in cement harbour courts filled with sea water, to professional basketball, handball, water-polo, tennis and soccer, especially the atmosphere in and around Maksimir Stadium when Hajduk Split visits Dinamo Zagreb, when the Torcida and Bad Blue Boys clash on the terraces, and when they leave afterwards in absolutely choked trams dispatched for free from around the city.

But all this waits for another book, and for another writer. I will enjoy Croatia rather than write about it. Now I can better assess the impact of these journeys on my sense of the country as another in which to live besides the one where I was born. My double identity has been entrenched more than ever, and the intricacies in the word "home," which I understood in passing but not intimately, have become privileged in my mind. Like many people, I know a home is more than the physical or psychical city, province or nation of a person's birth, more than the symbolic value of flags, anthems, insignias, or the comforts of a familiar language. Canada as home seems more fraught with complications than it did before. As one writer put it, "perhaps there's no return for anyone to a native land — only field notes for its reinvention."[1] For me home is really a complex of emotions and memories produced in that interface between myself and specific places not on maps. Thus a patch of ground is home in a way that a nation can never quite be. And yet at some point Srebrnjak will probably enter my psyche permanently and die "on the outside" when it no longer resembles itself when I lived there. Then for a while it will linger as a separate entity, no longer part of real space. Unlike some people, I seem able to accommodate a few such patches of personal ground, but my urge to travel hints that none of these satisfies me absolutely, that I'm still looking for one that does, or that it's become my nature to keep looking for something that (I suspect) doesn't exist.

My travels through Croatia have also made me deal early on with the banal (but shocking) reality of my own final "home" (in a place still unknown). Every step I took, every journey, was a repudiation of that reality. Travel itself is about living, searching out the requirements of life, whether physical or emotional; it is about moving, not delaying or waiting for fate. To rest is to die. And yet every journey is a death in an undiscovered country, a trip that will efface the traveller's former self. With every return, I shed my skin and am born anew. For the nomad, home is a provisional state in which the self absorbs the world, not the world the self. On the road my only home is me.

Now, across space and time, I hear a panoply of voices telling the story of the Croats, a story more optimistic than tragic, of a people who are survivors and, above all, realists. I hear voices of those who still labour on the land and at sea as before and under the same sun as their ancestors, who know this life won't continue forever, like their own. They've been too close to the seasons' cycles to be egotistical about their legacies, and know the value of living in the moment, not in the future or even in the past as their lives may suggest. I hear the voice of Petar Hektorović in his *Fishing and Fishermen's Conversations*:

> Reading, I came upon a fine thought from the wise:
> That without change nought may endure for long,
> And that much labour that is arduous
> Shall lead a man to death by its fatigue
> And that 'tis prudent who thinks not suddenly to fade,
> Avoiding labour to rest from hard travail
> That bringeth harm to body and to life,
> Opposing strength, the consciousness and skill
> And so they write: from labour find repose
> Who hasteneth not so to cut short his life.[2]

NOTES

2 ■ ZAGREB: THE TRANSFORMED CITY

1   Robert Kaplan, *Balkan Ghosts: A Journey Through History* (New York: Vintage Departures, 1994), xxvii.

2   Zvonomir Milcec, *Povratak Bana: Spomenik hrvatskog ponosa; hrvatskog sram* (Zagreb: Bookovoac, 1990) 7. The statue was unveiled for the first time on November 16, 1866. Its Viennese architect, Anton Dominik Fernkorn, died twelve years to the day afterward.

3   Marcus Tanner, *Croatia: A Nation Forged in War* (New Haven: Yale University Press, 1997), 87.

4   Count Louis Voinovitch, *Dalmatia and the Jugoslav Movement* (London: George Allen and Unwin Ltd., 1920), 151.

5   This, according to Ferdo Šišić, paraphrased by Ivan Babić, "Military History," in *Croatia: Land, People, Culture, Volume I,* eds. Francis H. Eterovich and Christopher Spalatin (Toronto: University of Toronto Press, 1964), 135. Babić goes on to claim that Batu Khan withdrew after heavy losses in Grobničko Polje, Trogir, and Klis. The death of the Great Khan (almost certainly the real reason for the withdrawal) is mentioned only as a coincidental event. Incorrectly, Babić says Genghis was the Great Khan in question (but he died around 1227, not 1242). For

more on Batu Khan's withdrawal from Croatia and his defeat at Trogir, see Chapter 8.

6 Stephen Gazi, *A History of Croatia* (New York: Barnes and Noble Books, 1993), 99.

7 The Croatia History Museum at the top of the old town near the Sabor testifies to the place conflict and war have in the country's "official" psychology. It's filled to the brim with swords, scabbards, daggers, muskets, pistols, and uniforms. The flag emblazoned with the *šahovnica*, which Jelačić allegedly carried during his inauguration as *ban*, is displayed in a glass case. Virtually all of the texts are in Croatian, a few in German. Notably, there are no translations. Croat history as shown here is essentially closed to outsiders—except of course to people of the former Yugoslavia, like the Serbs, who would understand almost everything. War is always more personal and bitter between former neighbours who understand the insult of each other's victories.

3 ■ PRIGORJE: THE GOOD AIR

1 John Berger, "On the Banks of the Sava," in *The Sense of Sight: Writings by John Berger*, ed. Lloyd Spencer (New York: Pantheon Books, 1985), 48–49.

2 A man in Brezje, Marijan Ratković, used to ring his old cow bell to trick his closest neighbours into thinking that the priest was coming, and made them rush around their houses getting everything ready.

3 Vladimir Dedijer, *Tito Speaks: His Self-Portrait and Struggle with Stalin* (London: Weidenfeld and Nicholson, 1953), 7.

4 ■ ZAGORJE: OF HEARTLANDS AND HAGIOGRAPHY

1 Drawing on a storehouse of stereotypes and clichés, some friendly, others acrimonious, Croats often typecast each other by region. A few of the stereotypes are older, while others appear determined by more recent history. According to people I spoke to in Prigorje, Slavonians eat well, have a way with horses, and love tamburica music; Dalmatians are good-looking, arrogant, and lazy; Herzegovinians are ambitious and tribal. While not unique among nations, such regionalism still functions in Croatia's discourse of self-representation. One could argue that it both divides the country and actually strengthens its sense of national identity.

2 For more on the zadruga and its decline, see *Communal Families in the Balkans: The Zadruga: Essays by Philip E. Mosely and Essays in His Honor*, ed. Robert F. Byrne (Notre Dame, Indiana: University of Notre Dame Press, 1976); Vera St. Erlich, *Family in Transition: A Study of 300 Yugoslav Villages* (Princeton: Princeton University Press, 1966); Jozo Tomasevich, *Peasants, Politics, and Economic Change in Yugoslavia* (Stanford: Stanford University Press, 1955); Ruth

Trouton, *Peasant Renaissance in Yugoslavia 1900–1950* (London: Routledge & Kegan Paul, 1952).

3   Dedijer, 4–5.

4   Viktor Horvat, *The Croatian Village Community in Yugoslavia* (PhD dissertation, Cornell University, 1929), 27.

5   Brian Hall, *The Impossible Country: A Journey Through the Last Days of Yugoslavia* (Boston: David R. Godine, 1994), 91.

6   Curiously, Gaj's legacy is sullied like Tito's and Tudjman's. In exchange for continued support for Illyrianism from Serbia's Karadjordjević dynasty, Gaj agreed to influence local authorities to arrest Prince Miloš of Serbia's exiled Obrenović dynasty during his travel through Croatia and have him executed. Even though Gaj had no stomach for murder, he liked money. For a price, he let the Prince go and was later accused of being at the bidding of "foreign" powers.

5 ■ SLAVONIA, POSAVINA: RETURN OF THE STORKS

1   Croats divide one of their three main dialects, *štokavski*, into three subgroups: *ijekavski* (*mlijeko* [milk]), *ikavski* (*mliko*), and *ekavski* (*mleko*). The other two dialects are *kajkavski* (spoken in northern Croatia) and *čakavski* (spoken on the coast). *Kaj, ča,* and *što* all mean "what." As Brian Hall put it, "Croats would tell me that Ijekavian is a distinguishing mark of Croatian, and Ekavian is a mark of Serbian. But this is absurd. The Serbs in the Krajina speak Ijekavian just like the Croat neighbors they are trying to kill." *The Impossible Country: A Journey Through the Last Days of Yugoslavia* (Boston: David R. Godine, Publisher, 1994), 40.

2   Stephen Raditch, "Autobiography of Stephen Raditch," (trans. *Current History*), *Current History* (October 1928): 106.

3   Raditch, 85–86.

4   Misha Glenny, *The Balkans: Nationalism, War and the Great Powers, 1804–1999* (New York: Viking, 2000), 260.

5   Goldstein, 101.

6   Šušak (1945–1998) was a western Herzegovinian and former pizza entrepreneur in Ottawa who helped procure funds for Tudjman's HDZ from the Croat diaspora. He later became defense minister. He forced Reihl-Kir to lead him and his men on a raid to the outskirts of Borovo Selo, where they fired three shoulder-launched missiles at the Serb sector of town. No one was killed in the attacks, but they were a clear provocation to the Serbs and only escalated tensions.

7   Laura Silber and Allan Little, *The Death of Yugoslavia* (London: Penguin/BBC Books, 1995), 157.

8   Silber and Little, 196.

6 ■ THE KVARNER ISLANDS: KRK, RAB

1 Rebecca West, *Black Lamb and Grey Falcon: A Journey through Yugoslavia* (New York: The Viking Press, 1941), 119.

2 Catherine Bracewell, *The Uskoks of Senj: Piracy, Banditry and Holy War in the Sixteenth-Century Adriatic* (New York: Cornell University Press, 1992), 157.

3 As historians have noted, in Croatia's mountainous hinterland to the north and south of Senj, the so-called Dinaric patriarchy was more prominent than the zadruga. Determined partly by the paucity of arable land, this peasant culture was more pastoral than sedentary. The Dinaric man is usually identified as Serb, not Croat. According to one Serb historian who wrote at a time of rising Serb nationalism in the early 1900s, Dinaric man displayed a "high sense of honor, mutual support for his fellow man, heroism, upholding of tradition, intensive national pride, and constructiveness in a political sense" (quoted in Tomasevich, 194). Not surprisingly, Croat historians tend to differ. One called Dinaric men "nomadic or seminomadic warlike sheep raisers and robbers in which power seeking ... is the main moving force," and he added that while the foundation of their social organization was zadruga-like, it was tribal, authoritarian, and less democratic than the Croat version (Tomasevich, 195).

4 Dominis was also Bishop of Senj and Archbishop of Split. His rift with the Catholic church led to his exile to England. He embraced Catholicism again and returned to Italy, only to be imprisoned in the Castle of St. Angelo by Pope Urban VIII, who reneged on his predecessor's pardon, and had Dominis' body burned upon his death.

8 ■ DALMATIA: BLACK VULTURE, OLD WANDERER

1 Dubravko Horvatic, *Croatia*, trans. Irena Zubcevic and Vera Krajski (Zagreb: Turistkomerc, 1992), 132.

2 Robert Hitchens, *The Near East: Dalmatia, Greece and Constantinople* (New York: The Century Company, 1913), 12.

3 John Berger, "On the Banks of the Sava," *The Sense of Sight: Writings by John Berger*, ed. Lloyd Spencer (New York: Pantheon Books, 1985), 49.

9 ■ DALMATIAN ISLANDS: HVAR, BRAČ, KORČULA

1 E.D. Goy, "Hektorović and His 'Ribanje'," *British-Croatia Review* 15 (January 1979): 6.

2 Edward A. Freeman, *Sketches From the Subject and Neighbour Lands of Venice* (London: MacMillan and Co., 1881), 203.

10 ■ DUBROVNIK: THE MAD MUSE

1 West, 233.

2 Willy Bachich, "Maritime History of the Eastern Adriatic," *Croatia: Land, People, Culture, Volume II*, eds. Francis H. Eterovich and Christopher Spalatin (Toronto: University of Toronto Press, 1964), 132–33.

11 ■ KRAJINA/HERZEGOVINA: THE ZONES

1 If Gypsies had been subject to victimization over the centuries, they had found in animals weaker others to victimize in turn, deflecting accusations of cruelty by blaming non-gypsies for giving them no other choice.

2 Long before, the region of Kordun was another military zone designed by the Hapsburgs as so-called ramparts of Christendom. The name Kordun derives from Hapsburg ruler Maria Theresa's *cordon sanitaire*, a line of wooden border posts established in 1770 to prevent the spread of plague by interning travellers and disinfecting their possessions with vinegar (Tanner, 59).

3 Paul Blanchard, *Blue Guide Yugoslavia* (London: A and C Black, 1989), 365. To "make the paradox even greater," writes Goldstein, the bridge had been built "under the direction of Muslim architects, by Croatian stone-masons from Dubrovnik and Korčula skilled in making such sophisticated structures" (246–47).

4 Reconstruction began in 2001.

12 ■ ISTRIA: THE GENTLE CLIMATE

1 Thus, the assumption that the Istro-Romanians are directly linked to Romania proper may be more wishful thinking than truth. See Noel Malcolm, *Bosnia: A Short History* (Washington Square, New York: New York University Press, 1996), 73–81.

2 Richard Ellmann, *James Joyce* (New York: Oxford University Press, 1982), 192; my emphasis.

3 Ellmann, 192.

CONCLUSION

1 James Clifford, *The Predicament of Culture: Twentieth-Century Ethnography* (Cambridge, MA: Harvard University Press, 1988), 173.

2 Petar Hektorović, "Fishing and Fishermens' Conversations," trans. E.D. Goy, *British-Croatia Review* 15 (January 1979): 14.

■ BIBLIOGRAPHY

Babić, Ivan. "Military History." *In Croatia: Land, People, Culture, Volume I*. Francis H. Eterovich and Christopher Spalatin, eds. Toronto: University of Toronto Press, 1964. 131–66.

Bachich, Willy. "Maritime History of the Eastern Adriatic." *Croatia: Land, People, Culture, Volume II*. Francis H. Eterovich and Christopher Spalatin, eds. Toronto: University of Toronto Press, 1964.

Blanchard, Paul. *Blue Guide Yugoslavia*. London: A & C Black, 1989.

Berger, John. "On the Banks of the Sava." *The Sense of Sight: Writings by John Berger*. New York: Pantheon Books, 1985. 45–49.

Bracewell, Catherine Wendy. *The Uskoks of Senj: Piracy, Banditry and Holy War in the Sixteenth-Century Adriatic*. New York: Cornell University Press, 1992.

Clifford, James. *The Predicament of Culture: Twentieth-Century Ethnography*. Cambridge, MA: Harvard University Press, 1988.

Dedijer, Vladimir. *Tito Speaks: His Self-Portrait and Struggle with Stalin*. London: Weidenfeld and Nicholson, 1953.

Ellman, Richard. *James Joyce*. New York: Oxford University Press, 1982.

Freeman, Edward A. *Sketches From the Subject and Neighbour Lands of Venice*. London: MacMillan and Co., 1881.

Gazi, Stephen. *A History of Croatia*. New York: Barnes and Noble Books, 1993.

Glenny, Misha. *The Balkans: Nationalism, War and the Great Powers, 1804–1999*. New York: Viking, 2000.

Goldstein, Ivo. *Croatia: A History*. Trans. Nikolina Jovanovic. Montreal: McGill-Queen's University Press, 1999.

Goy, E.D. "Hektorović and His 'Ribanje'." *British-Croatia Review* 15 (January 1979): 3–11.

Hall, Brian. *The Impossible Country: A Journey Through the Last Days of Yugoslavia*. Boston: David R. Godine, Publisher, 1994.

Hektorović, Petar. *Fishing and Fishermen's Conversations*. Trans. E.D. Goy. *British-Croatia Review* 15 (January, 1979): 13–46.

Horvat, Viktor. "The Croatian Village Community in Yugoslavia." PhD dissertation. Ithaca: Cornell University, 1929.

Horvatic, Dubravko. *Croatia*. Trans. Irena Zubcevic and Vera Krnajski. Zagreb: Tursitkomerc, 1992.

Kaplan, Robert D. *Balkan Ghosts: A Journey Through History*. New York: Random House, 1993.

Malcolm, Noel. *Bosnia: A Short History*. Washington Square, New York: New York University Press, 1996.

Raditch, Stephen. "Autobiography of Stephen Raditch." (Trans. *Current History*.) *Current History* (October 1928): 82–106.

Silber, Laura and Allan Little. *The Death of Yugoslavia*. London: Penguin/BBC Books, 1995.

Tanner, Marcus. *Croatia: A Nation Forged by War*. New Haven and London: Yale University Press, 1997.

Tomasevich, Jozo. *Politics and Economics Change in Yugoslavia*. Stanford: Stanford University Press, 1855.

Voinovitch, Count Louis. *Dalmatia and the Jugoslav Movement*. London: George Allen and Unwin Ltd., 1920.

West, Rebecca. *Black Lamb and Grey Falcon: A Journey Through Yugoslavia*. New York: The Viking Press, 1941.

◨ INDEX

Note: Page numbers for illustrations are in italics.